State of the Urban Youth 2010/11

Leveling the Playing Field:
Inequality of Youth Opportunity

UN⊕HABITAT

Foreword

Never have so many young people around the world been so healthy and literate, but the opportunities attached to the unprecedented prosperity of our cities keep eluding too many of them. That so many of those in charge of our collective future are denied the right to fulfilling lives and remain consigned to the sordid urban dead ends known as slums comes as a major challenge to sustainable development policies.

At this unique juncture in history where half of humankind is under 25 years of age, youth exclusion features as a major aspect of the "urban divide" that gives its theme to UN-HABITAT's 2010/11 State of the World Cities report. What experts refer to as the "youth bulge" in today's global demography is as good an opportunity as any to launch this companion State of Urban Youth report which, from now on and every other year, will sharpen the more general focus of the main flagship report.

This Youth Report, the first of its kind, comes in response to calls from young peoples' organizations across the world. The fact that these requests were heard, and subsequently endorsed by an attentive Governing Council in 2009, is testament to this organization's, and more generally the UN system's, ability to respond to emerging global challenges with an appropriate mix of well-informed analysis and realistic policy recommendations.

As is the case with the main State of the World Cities document, the analysis in this Youth Report combines the latest available policy and academic research with the opinions voiced by well-selected local focus groups in a number of representative cities. This cross-regional survey of five cities where a gaping "urban divide" urgently needs bridging also scrutinizes the determinants of youth opportunity and inequality. The main finding is that unequal access is a phenomenon that begins in childhood and continues into youth, and then into adulthood through inequality in income, employment and housing.

Consistent with the "rights-based" approach endorsed in the main report, the five-city survey reflects local young people's perceptions of the extent to which the "right to the city" is effective in its four dimensions – political, economic, social and cultural – in their respective day-to-day environments. Survey returns suggest that persistent inequality of opportunity deprives youth of their rights to the city, and that promoting equal access to shelter, education and services results in more stable and cohesive societies. Education appears as a major determinant of equal opportunities, and the "right to the city" is more effective for those who have access to services and education early in life.

Equality of opportunity requires a "leveling of the playing field", so that circumstances that are beyond an individual's control do not adversely influence her/his life chances. Predetermined circumstances such as gender, parents' education, father's occupation and the location where one was brought up determine outcome opportunities in adulthood.

This Report confirms that more education results in more opportunities. Access to school is largely determined by economic factors (costs) that ultimately depend on political will (fee exemptions, etc.). Just as relevant is the quality of education, which can also be affected by predetermined factors like class, race and social status.

Like the main report, this one also confirms the negative role of gender disparities in education. Following from the findings, this Report makes a number of policy recommendations. These include a call on governments to allocate more resources to education and to target special support at underprivileged and more vulnerable groups. The Report also advocates a review of those Millennium Development Goals that address young people and education.

Another major finding in this Report is that access to land and safe urban space is important for the protection, voice and empowerment of young people, it calls on public authorities to meet these needs for safe peer exchange. The findings in this Report also have a significant potential bearing on UN-HABITAT'S own youth policies and programmes. Taking advantage of training and education opportunities represents both an acquisition of skills and a capacity builder for urban youth. The main challenge for youth training programmes has to do with the way young people market and use skills once they have acquired them.

In its own effort to broaden the scope of opportunities for underprivileged urban youth around the world, UN-HABITAT is extending the reach of its partnerships beyond local authorities and civil society. With its recently-launched Opportunities Fund for Youth-Led Development, our organization supports dynamic young individuals who demonstrate the determination to put their entrepreneurial skills at the service of local communities – in the process helping to pave the way for environmentally and socially sustainable, inclusive cities.

Since humankind today is younger than it has ever been, our collective future will, more than ever, be shaped by today's youth. In this sense, this fledgling 21st century belongs to young people. If we want our, the older generation's, legacy to endure for the decades to come, let us make sure that we pass it on to those billions of able young hands that are only waiting for the opportunity.

Anna K. Tibaijuka
Under-Secretary-General and Executive Director
United Nations Human Settlements Programme
(UN-HABITAT)

Acknowledgements

Core Team
Director: Oyebanji Oyeyinka
Coordinators: Subramonia Ananthakrishnan, Mutinta Munyati
Statistical Adviser: Gora Mboup

Principal Author: Oyebanji Oyeyinka

Contributors: Catherine Adeya, Boladale A. Adebowale, Jennifer Jones, Padma Prakash,
Sunita Kapila, Kaushalesh Lal, Gora Mboup, Pedro Strozenberg

Editorial Team:
Guenter Karl, Eduardo Lopez Moreno, Thierry Naudin,
Darcy Varney, Paul Wambua

Support team
Statistics: Julius Majale, Philip Mukungu, James Wang'ombe
Administrative Assistance: Esther Naibei

Design and layout: Andrew Ondoo, Paul Wambua

Cover images: **Top:** Youth centre; space provided by the City Council of Nairobi, Kenya © UN-HABITAT
Bottom Left: Unequal playing fields…young players in action at the V. Youth Football Festival,
Kaposvar, Hungary © Muzsy/Shutterstock
Bottom Right: Unequal playing fields…children playing football in Kibera, Kenya
© Nairobi River Basin Project/UNEP
Back cover: Favela in Rio de Janeiro, Brazil © Gary Yim/Shutterstock

Sponsor: Government of Norway

Printer: Earthscan

Contents

03:Family Resources as Drivers of Opportunity Inequality

04:Young People's Right to Equal Opportunities in the City

05:Leveling the Playing Field: Rights and Equal Opportunities for Youth

"In most Brazilian cities the poverty is not in your face but in Rio it is..." Jorge Bittar, Rio de Janeiro's Municipal Secretary © **Mauricio Hora**

A summary profile of the five cities under review

This report is based on data from UN-HABITAT's *Global Urban Indicator Database*, as well as surveys of, and focus group discussions with, selected representative groups of young people in five major cities located in four developing regions: Rio de Janeiro (Brazil), Mumbai (India), Kingston (Jamaica), Nairobi (Kenya) and Lagos (Nigeria). The following is a summary profile of the countries and cities under review.

The population of **Brazil** is estimated in 2010 at 195 million[1] with a density[2] of 22.4 per sq. km. The urban population was 163 million in 2007, with 28 per cent (or 45.7 million) living in slums[3]. **Rio de Janeiro** is the second largest city in Brazil with an approximate population of 6.1 million[4]. The youth population in Brazil (10-24 years) is 51.7 million, which is 27 per cent of the total[5]. Rio is host to approximately 1 million young people (between 15 and 24 years old), or 17.4 per cent of the total[6].

Rio de Janeiro is also known for its *"favelas"*.[7] These can be traced to the end of the 19th century with the abolition of slavery and with rural migration. There are over 1,000 favelas in the city, housing approximately 20 per cent of the total population[8].

Brazil's GDP per capita is equivalent to US $4,274, and Rio contributes 5.5 per cent to the aggregate figure. The city ranks second nationally for industrial production and financial services, trailing only São Paulo. Having been the federal capital before Brasilia took over, metropolitan Rio is still host to many corporate headquarters[9].

By comparison with nationwide averages, the city enjoys high rates of education and employment[10], which partly conceal high degrees of income/consumption inequality.[11]

India is one of the most populous nations in the world, being host to approximately 1.21 billion[12] in 2010, with a population density of 378.3 per sq. km[13]. The urban population is 341 million, of which 32.1 per cent (or 109 million) live in slums[14]. **Mumbai** is the capital of Maharashtra, a large highly industrialized, progressive state which until a decade ago reported remarkable progress on social and economic indices.

India's GDP per capita is equivalent to US $686[15], but it is three times as high in Mumbai, the country's business capital. Under the British Protectorate, Mumbai owed its development as a commercial, trade and communication hub to its strategic location. With the advent of textile mills in the 19th century, Mumbai also attracted rural migrants from the hinterland and from across India, making up the blend of regional, linguistic, ethnic and class diversity that remains its defining feature.

Jamaica has an estimated population of 2.7 million[16] (density[17]: 247.1 per sq. km) in 2010, of which 50 per cent are urban. The proportion of urban residents living in slum areas is 60 per cent (or 855,000).[18] **Kingston**, Jamaica's capital city, was host to 666,200 people in 2008, or a quarter of Jamaica's total population. The country's youth (10-24 years) numbers 800,000[19], or some 30 per cent of the total population.

Jamaica's GDP per capita is US $3,861[20]. Kingston is a busy port – the seventh largest in the world. Downtown on the harbour are many of the poorest areas, including slum communities. The share of the wealthiest quintile in national consumption has remained stable at around 45 per cent since 1990, while the share of the poorest quintile has remained between 6 and 7 per cent, suggesting that economic exclusion in Jamaica is entrenched. The services sector is becoming more and more dominant, employing 65 per cent of the labour force in 2008. Kingston has the highest concentration of labour, with a quarter of the country's population but a third of its labour force.

The total population of **Kenya** stood at 28 million by the latest available (1999) census, of which 2.1 million in the capital, **Nairobi**. The 2010 nationwide estimate is 40 million[21], with a population density[22] of 65.9 per sq. km. The urban population was about 8 million in 2007, of which 54.8 per cent (or 4.3 million) live in slums[23]. Today, estimates are that Nairobi alone is host to over 4 million. The youth population (10-24 years) is 12.2 million, or 35 per cent of the nation's total[24]. At the time this Report went to print, the results of Kenya's most recent census (concluded in August 2009) were yet to be published.

Kenya's GDP per capita is US $459[25]. Nairobi is an international, regional, national and local hub for commerce, transport, culture, regional cooperation and economic development. As many as 25 per cent of the national labour force and 43 per cent of total urban workers are employed in Nairobi, which generates over 45 per cent of Kenya's GDP[26]. Nairobi features one of the highest annual growth rates of all other cities in Africa.

The population of **Nigeria** in 2010 is estimated at 158 million[27] with a density[28] of 162.5 per sq. km. Youth (10-24 years) account for over 34 per cent (or 45.4 million) of the total[29]. Nearly half the country's population (or 70.5 million) lived in urban areas in 2007, of which 64.2 per cent (or 45.3 million) in slums[30].

Lagos stands as the most populous city in Nigeria, being host to 36.8 per cent of the total urban population. The precise demographic data for Lagos is highly controversial, as the Lagos state's population of 9 million[31] is deemed to be grossly underestimated. The Lagos state government maintains that its population is not inferior to 17.5 million. The United Nations estimates that at its present growth rate of 6-8 per cent, Lagos state will be the third largest mega-city in the world by 2015 (after Tokyo and Mumbai), with a population of over 25 million[32].

Nigeria's GDP per capita is equivalent to US $473.[33] Lagos is the country's commercial and economic capital, and is host to the regional headquarters of many international firms. From an ethnic point of view, the city is like Nigeria in miniature as about every ethnic group in the country is represented there.[34]

END NOTES

[1] UN DESA, 2008.
[2] World Bank, 2009.
[3] UN-HABITAT, 2009.
[4] Instituto Pereira Passos, 2008 [Accessed Aug. 2009 from http://www.armazemdedados.rio.rj.gov.br]
[5] Population reference Bureau, 2009.
[6] National Homes Survey – PNAD, 2003 – IBGE
[7] "Favela" refers to poor urban neighbourhoods or shanty towns.
[8] Figures from Instituto Pereira Passos [Accessed Aug. 2009 at http://www.armezemdedados.rio.rj.gov.br]
[9] Accessed Dec. 2009 from http://en.wikipedia.org/wiki/Rio_de_Janeiro

[10] Ibid. Average net enrolment ratio (primary and secondary): 95%; unemployment rate: just under 10% of the labour force.
[11] Ibid. (accessed March 2009). In the year 2000, Rio's Gini coefficient stood at 0.62, denoting "very high rates" of inequality.
[12] UN DESA, 2008.
[13] World Bank, 2009.
[14] UN-HABITAT, 2009.
[15] World Bank, 2009.
[16] UN DESA, 2008-.
[17] World Bank, 2009.
[18] UN-HABITAT, 2009.
[19] Population Reference Bureau, 2009.

[20] World Bank, 2009.
[21] UN DESA, 2008.
[22] World Bank 2009.
[23] UN-HABITAT, 2009.
[24] Population Reference Bureau, 2009.
[25] World Bank, 2009.
[26] UN-HABITAT, 2006.
[27] UN DESA, 2008.
[28] World Bank, 2009.
[29] Population Reference Bureau, 2009.
[30] UN-HABITAT, 2009.
[31] Federal Office of Statistics, 2006.
[32] Accessed Aug. 2009 from http://www.TheFirstGroup.com
[33] World Bank, 2009.
[34] Roberts & Oladeji, 2001:1.

Background Data on the Countries under Review

GROSS ENROLMENT RATIO (PRIMARY) 2007

BRAZIL	137
INDIA	112
JAMAICA	95
KENYA	106
NIGERIA	97

Source: World Bank (2009)

NET ENROLMENT RATIO (PRIMARY) 2007

BRAZIL	94
INDIA	89
JAMAICA	90
KENYA	75
NIGERIA	63

Source: World Bank (2009)

GROSS ENROLMENT RATIO (SECONDARY) 2007

BRAZIL	105
INDIA	55
JAMAICA	87
KENYA	50
NIGERIA	32

Source: World Bank (2009)

NET ENROLMENT RATIO (SECONDARY) 2007

BRAZIL	79
INDIA	NOT AVAILABLE
JAMAICA	78
KENYA	43
NIGERIA	N/A

Source: World Bank (2009)

GROSS ENROLMENT RATIO (TERTIARY) 2007

BRAZIL	25
INDIA	12
JAMAICA	N/A
KENYA	N/A
NIGERIA	10

Source: World Bank (2009)

YOUTH POPULATION AGED 10-24 – 2006

BRAZIL	51,700,000
INDIA	331,100,000
JAMAICA	800,000
KENYA	12,200,000
NIGERIA	45,400,000

Source: Population Reference Bureau (2009)

YOUTH POPULATION AGED 10-24 (% OF TOTAL) 2006

BRAZIL	27
INDIA	30
JAMAICA	30
KENYA	35
NIGERIA	34

Source: Population Reference Bureau (2009)

POPULATION DENSITY 2007 (PER SQUARE KM)

BRAZIL	22.4
INDIA	378.3
JAMAICA	247.1
KENYA	65.9
NIGERIA	162.5

Source: World Bank (2009)

URBAN POPULATION AT MID-YEAR BY MAJOR AREA, REGION AND COUNTRY (THOUSANDS)

	1990	1995	2000	2005	2007
BRAZIL	111,851	125,685	141,404	157,369	163,462
INDIA	219,758	253,774	289,438	325,563	341,247
JAMAICA	1,171	1,258	1,342	1,413	1,439
KENYA	4,273	5,193	6,167	7,384	7,982
NIGERIA	33,325	42,372	53,048	65,270	70,539

Source: UN-HABITAT (2010c)

PROPORTION OF URBAN POPULATION LIVING IN SLUM AREAS (%)

	1990	1995	2000	2005	2007
BRAZIL	36.7	34.1	31.5	29	28
INDIA	54.9	48.2	41.5	34.8	32.1
JAMAICA	N/A	N/A	N/A	60.5	N/A
KENYA	54.9	54.8	54.8	54.8	54.8
NIGERIA	77.3	73.5	69.6	65.8	64.2

Source: UN-HABITAT (2010c)

URBAN SLUM POPULATION AT MID-YEAR BY MAJOR AREA, REGION AND COUNTRY (THOUSANDS)

	1990	1995	2000	2005	2007
BRAZIL	40,998	42,856	44,601	45,613	45,708
INDIA	120,746	122,376	120,117	113,223	109,501
JAMAICA	N/A	N/A	N/A	855	N/A
KENYA	2,345	2,848	3,379	4,044	4,370
NIGERIA	25,763	31,127	36,930	42,928	45,309

Source: UN-HABITAT (2010c)

GDP 2007 (CONSTANT 2000 US$) (BILLION)

BRAZIL	812, 6
INDIA	771,1
JAMAICA	10,3
KENYA	17,2
NIGERIA	69,9

Source: World Bank (2009)

GDP PER CAPITA, 2007 (CONSTANT 2000 US$)

BRAZIL	4,273.97
INDIA	685.55
JAMAICA	3,861.50
KENYA	459.58
NIGERIA	472.90

Source: World Bank (2009)

Key Findings of the Report

This Report is based on a survey of the historical and generational determinants of youth opportunity inequality and deprivation across different interconnected spheres of urban activity in five representative cities in four developing regions (Africa, Asia, Latin America and the Caribbean). The survey results strongly suggest that the degree of outcome inequality (such as earnings and assets) that defines youth exclusion or inclusion in urban life is highly related to the (un)equal opportunities that occur in successive life stages.

Unequal access often begins in childhood and continues into youth and adulthood, perpetuating the disadvantage faced in the early years. Inequality in access to basic education as well as the quality of schooling often leads to opportunity deprivations in terms of income, employment and housing. Unequal opportunities exacerbate exposure to the risk factors that undermine young people's development into responsible, accomplished adults. In the long term, persistent and subsequent intergenerational inequity deprives youth of their political, economic, social and cultural rights to the city. The nurturing and protection of young people through equal access to shelter, education and services during childhood and the transition to adulthood is a capital investment that is essential to stable and cohesive societies.

Equality of opportunity requires a leveling of the playing field so that circumstances that are beyond the control of an individual do not adversely influence their life chances. The following are the key findings of this *State of the Urban Youth 2010/11.*

1. Predetermined circumstances impact on youth inequality of opportunity

These are issues that a young person has no control over but which exert life-determining effects on the trajectory of their outcome opportunities as adults. These factors are critical to eventual opportunity outcomes. Predetermined circumstances include gender, parents' education, father's occupation as well as the location where an individual grew up.

2. Education is a key determinant of opportunity equality

According to the UN-HABITAT 2009 Urban Youth Survey, cities offer young people with higher levels of education greater opportunities to integrate into urban life than they do for the less educated. These findings point to education, especially for females, as a key driver in accessing the opportunities that come with urban life and taking advantage of them.

3. Inequality is, to a significant extent, determined by the quality of education

Outcome inequality is to a significant extent determined by the quality of education. Inequality of educational opportunity obtains when the quality of education available to children is determined by an individual's class, gender, race or social status. A broad set of family resource factors, such as location of home (slum vs. non-slum), income and father's earnings contribute to compound social inequality.

4. Opportunity inequality is driven by asymmetric political structures

Schooling and institutions regulating access to enrolment in developing countries to some extent contribute to the class and social divide in urban areas. Educational opportunity is driven by unequal and asymmetric political decisionmaking structures whereby youth from poorer backgrounds tend to bear the brunt of national and local policies. According to the UN-HABITAT survey across the five cities under review, 60 per cent of youth with primary level education are denied equality of opportunity, compared with over 40 per cent of university-educated youth, with children from slums and poor backgrounds the most affected. Availability of schools in urban areas does not automatically result in higher enrolment numbers. Families in slum communities often cannot afford school because the combined cost of fees, textbooks and uniforms is prohibitive.

5. Gender disparities in educational achievement lead to unequal opportunities

Gender disparities in educational attainment persist at the secondary and tertiary levels. There are also disparities in school drop-out rates, with young women predominating due (largely) to adolescent pregnancies as well as socio-cultural pressures against continuing education to higher levels. There is a negative relationship between female secondary enrolment in 1990 and income inequality in 2005. In other words, early investment in female education can directly reduce income inequality in later stages.

6. Higher enrolment numbers in 1990 lead to lower inequalities in 2005

Macroeconomic analysis shows that countries with higher levels of primary, secondary and tertiary enrolment tend to record lower degrees of income inequality 15 years later.

7. Higher primary enrolment ratios in 1990 boost GDP in 2005

Relatively higher primary enrolment ratios in 1990 were found to affect gross domestic product (GDP) in 2005, which in turn resulted in lower Gini coefficients of income/consumption disparities. The conclusion from UN-HABITAT research is that higher enrolment in primary, secondary and tertiary education leads to a reduction in income inequalities after a period of time.

8. Parents' education determines youth opportunity inequality

Parents' education, and particularly mothers', is a significant factor in youth educational and outcome opportunities. The UN-HABITAT survey shows that uneducated youth from poor homes and poor neighbourhoods (slums) tend to be the most excluded in their cities. Parents' low levels of education tend to perpetuate intergenerational underachievement. The UN-HABITAT survey found a strong relationship between girls' primary education and mothers' education in urban areas. Educated mothers promote their own children's education. However, the literacy gap between poor and rich households persists, largely due to skewed public spending by governments as well as to parents' asset deprivation.

9. Improved literacy rates have not resulted in proportional job opportunities

Improved literacy rates and educational achievement have not resulted in greater employment opportunities for young people. Millions are either jobless or in unproductive employment. Current statistics point to alarming numbers of "idle" youth, i.e., neither in school nor at work, in Latin America, Africa and Asia.

10. Education and early access to services make the "right to the city" more effective

Those young people who benefit from basic services during childhood tend to have access to better-quality primary education. They also tend to have the highest opportunities to access political office, and therefore take advantage of networks and social status to secure political opportunities.

Policy Recommendations

Policies must recognize youth as a period of identity-building and transition to responsible citizenship

If young people are effectively to move to responsible citizenship in their adult lives, they must be safe, healthy and engaged in a positive way in their transition years. Government must enshrine this vision in national plans and policies.

Youth-responsive policy and institutions require dedicated capacity-building among urban decisionmakers and youth

Local leaders, councillors, mayors and municipal officials require training in two crucial areas: (a) youth participation in strategic city planning and budgetary procedures, and (b) facilitating partnerships with major stakeholders.

Policies and resources must focus more on education, especially for young females

Significant gender disparities in secondary and tertiary (especially female) enrolment must be remedied by targeted public policies.

Review the Millennium Development Goals (MDGs) related to youth education targets

Ten years after the MDGs were first set, it is time for a review as far as young people are concerned, and to mobilize more resources.

Opportunity inequality should receive special attention

Institutional mechanisms must be set up to mitigate the disadvantages resulting from predetermined circumstances and reduce the effects of intergenerational inequity.

Match education and training to the skills in demand on the labour market

Providing youth with employable skills and decent work is a challenge for both the public and the private sectors, and non-formal delivery has a role to play.

Policy responses must espouse the multidimensional nature of youth opportunity

National sectoral policies do not address youth opportunity issues, even where youth are predominant in urban constituencies. Social inequalities in education and nutrition are certain to impair productive and other individual capacities. Responsiveness to youth needs across policy areas demands cross-sector coordination.

Collect systematic and consistent urban youth data

Most publicly available national surveys or indicators of well-being are based on household data but analyses of urban youth- specific issues are rare. This must be remedied, especially with regard to young people and other marginalized groups.

Access to land and safe urban space is important for the protection, voice and empowerment of urban youth

Young people need places where they are sheltered, protected and mentored into the democratic and economic processes, paving the way for a united urban youth lobby and support system.

Need for better health policies

Reducing inequality of opportunity will require better health policies and more resource allocation to healthcare; at the same time, inequality of health opportunities is largely determined by shelter conditions, and therefore can also be tackled though proportionally higher resources for reduction of shelter deprivation in slums.

Specific policies for Shelter deprivation

Policymakers must deploy differentiated policies that target the multidimensional nature of shelter deprivation and its interconnections with a variety of health and educational opportunity inequalities. For instance, a special Educational Fund should be set up for youth growing in slums, with special attention to girls' education.

UN-HABITAT'S Opportunities fund beneficiaries
© **UN-HABITAT**

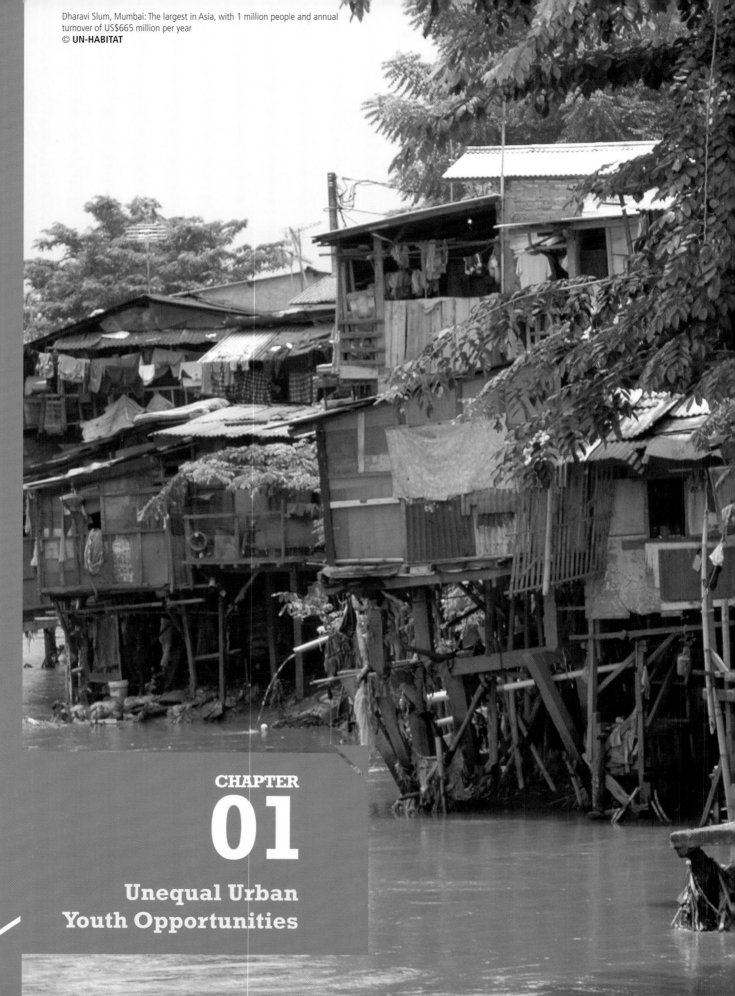

Dharavi Slum, Mumbai: The largest in Asia, with 1 million people and annual turnover of US$665 million per year
© UN-HABITAT

CHAPTER
01

Unequal Urban Youth Opportunities

> **"In the state of nature...all men are born equal, but they cannot continue in this equality. Society makes them lose it, and they recover it only by the protection of the law."**
> Charles de Montesquieu

1.0 Introduction

The universally accepted notions of justice, equity and fairness imply that every member of society is provided with a "level playing field" in terms of opportunities for the development of their potential and optimization of their welfare. Far from being an outcome, "equity" is a process built upon the concept of equal opportunity[1]. According to Roemer,[2] equity demands an "equal opportunity policy". He argues that although individuals bear some responsibility for their own welfare, they are also affected by circumstances over which they have no control. Public policy should, therefore, aim at equalizing "advantages" among people from groups with different circumstances, and increasing the "fairness" of social processes. If the outcomes then turn out to be unequal, they are still fair.

This *State of the Urban Youth 2010/2011*, the first of its kind, focuses largely on the unaddressed issue of inequality of opportunity in relation to the more widely known and equally important concept of inequality of outcome, that is, relative poverty.

The latter is usually measured in terms of consumption and income, while inequality of opportunity deals mostly with equity. The widening divide between the wealthiest and the poorest, and the increasing difficulty in achieving anticipated income convergence, suggest that development policies and interventions should take more seriously the targeting of opportunities for the most vulnerable in any given society. Policies must provide a "level playing field" for the more disadvantaged, including children, youth and women, an issue that is now taking on greater urgency in the development debate.

A growing body of literature over time[3] shows that predetermined circumstances over which an individual child or young person has no control over do exert a profound, life-determining impact on the trajectory of his or her outcome opportunities as an adult. These predetermined factors include gender, parents' education, father's occupation and the location where an individual grew up. These factors are critical to the eventual opportunity outcomes.

BOX 1.1 **EQUALITY, OPPORTUNITIES AND THE "LEVEL PLAYING FIELD"**

Equality refers to a situation where different people share at least one and the same characteristic feature. Similarity does not mean wholesale sameness, and this distinction is at the root of the principle of non-discrimination which in turn forms the basis of fundamental or human rights.

Subsuming as it does the notions of respect and non-discriminating treatment, equality has long been closely associated with justice and more specifically, for the past century or so, with what is now known as "distributive justice". This refers to the proper allocation of wealth, power, rewards, etc., between different people or groups thereof.

Inclusion refers to a non-discriminating dispensation across a whole community. Such non-discrimination also involves the possibility of individual self-fulfillment and exercise of one's capacities, which in turn largely depends on factors like family, education, health and social capital. These circumstances and factors combine with individual capacities to determine the opportunities a person will have in the course of their lives, and particularly during their early, formative years.

Equality of opportunity features prominently in contemporary theories of distributive justice. It calls for mitigation (through redistribution mechanisms) of those predetermined circumstances (gender, race, family background, education, etc.) over which a young person has no control, but which can hinder their chances of leading a fulfilling life. Such mitigation opens up a "level playing field" for all, privileged or underprivileged. It is then for individuals freely to choose whether and how to make the most of this "just" framework for interaction with society. Since equality of opportunity allows for differences in individual abilities, efforts and aspirations, it does not necessarily lead to equal outcomes – but these at least can be deemed to be fair.

Teenage girls enjoying their sewing class in Kabul, Afghanistan
© D. O'Reilly

For instance, access to clean water, sanitation, electricity and completion of high school respectively influence the quality of nutrition, health, ability to read and propensity to attain higher levels of education. Low levels of parental education tend to perpetuate intergenerational under-achievement. Recent findings show that between 25 and 50 per cent of the income inequality observed among adults in Latin America results from life circumstances faced at an early age.[4] Inequality of opportunity and inequality of outcome have accentuated the growth of non-inclusive and unequal cities.

This Report comes as a companion to UN-HABITAT's *State of the World's Cities 2010/2011*[5] which focuses on "Bridging the urban divide". That broader-encompassing report analyses the dynamics of economic growth and urban inequality, urban poverty and shelter deprivations within cities. The purpose of the report is to understand and appreciate the relationship between poverty, inequality, slum formation and economic growth, and in the next step to formulate and implement all-inclusive programmes and policies that can guide stakeholders in building inclusive and equal cities.

The *State of the World's Cities 2010/2011* defines an inclusive city as one with the following characteristics:

i. *Social Inclusion* provides all citizens regardless of race, ethnicity, gender or socio-economic status with adequate housing and decent basic services, facilitating equal access to social amenities and public goods that are essential to promote the general and environmental well-being of all residents.

ii. *Political Inclusion* protects citizens' rights and freedom, and promotes social and political participation that contributes to more relevant and democratic decision making.

iii. *Economic Inclusion* fosters economic development by way of equal opportunities for business development and access to employment, promoting pro-poor economic policies.

iv. *Cultural Inclusion* promotes social integration and celebrates diversity. It values people's cultural rights, recognizing the human capital of all segments of society, and looks to enhance them through creative expression.

1.1 Focus of this State of Urban Youth 2010/2011

The broad rationale behind this Youth Report is a systematic review of empirical evidence of unequal opportunities across selected cities in Africa, Latin America, the Caribbean and Asia. This involved a study of the institutional and organizational capacity underlying the four essential dimensions of equality: social, political, economic and cultural. The aim is to draw national and international attention to this very critical issue that has lasting and intergenerational implications for society.

1.2 Methodology and Analytical Framework

In order to achieve the above objectives, both quantitative and qualitative data collection methods were used in the study. Questionnaires helped to capture the four dimensions of equality as well as the institutional and organizational issues that are critical to effective equality and equity in five selected, representative cities: Kingston, Jamaica; Lagos, Nigeria; Nairobi, Kenya; Mumbai, India; and Rio de Janeiro, Brazil. Focus group discussions complemented answers to the questionnaire, involving 20 to 25 selected participants in each city. The quantitative data include the actual achievements of the various cities in the four areas of equality under focus, as perceived by the local young people who participated in the survey and the focus groups.

The analytical framework behind this Report is depicted in Figure 1.1. The variables used in the framework are grouped into the following four main factors:

- Predetermined Circumstances
- Family Resources and Location
- Intergenerational Inequalities
- Inequality of Opportunities

These factors are used to identify and analyse the variables that affect the four essential dimensions of inclusiveness and equality in cities. The actual variables used in the analysis are listed in Table 1.1.

In Table 1.1, "Predetermined Circumstances" involves variables such as gender and caste. These are determined by birth, and in normal circumstances they remain unchanged.

FIGURE 1.1: **THE ANALYTICAL FRAMEWORK**

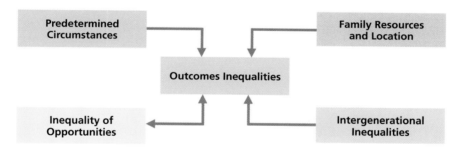

TABLE 1.1: **VARIABLES USED IN THE UN-HABITAT URBAN YOUTH SURVEY 2009**

Factor	Variables
Predetermined Circumstances	Sex of respondent
	Race, ethnicity, caste, disability, etc.
Family Resources and Location	Childhood residence
	Access to basic services (health care, electricity, water and sanitation)
Intergenerational Inequalities	Father's education
	Mother's education
Inequality of Opportunities	Quality of primary education
	Educational attainment of respondents

Source: UN-HABITAT, 2009

Youth from different parts of the world on International Youth Day, 2007, Nairobi, Kenya © **UN-HABITAT**

Gender, family wealth and quality of education are considered to be further determinants of inequality of opportunity.

In this Report, predetermined circumstances like gender and caste are exogenous to the respondents and are expected to affect practically all the four types of inequalities, both positively or negatively. For instance, de Barros *et al.* [6] show that in Latin America and the Caribbean, ethnicity and birthplace are not strong determinants of unequal economic opportunity. Family background variables, such as parents' education and father's occupation, are predominant. Education features as a major factor behind the unequal outcomes evidenced in this Report and therefore requires closer attention, including its strong connection to gender (see Box 1.2).

These circumstances can influence inequality but the reverse does not hold. In this Report, "Family Resources and Location" includes variables that can negatively or positively affect the degree of a family's social inclusion, namely: "Childhood Residence" and "Access to Basic Facilities" such as electricity, tenure, health care, water and sanitation.

The third factor is the "Intergenerational Inequalities", i.e., any disparities that are related to individual families and are passed on from one generation to another. These include parents' education and income levels. Finally, the "Inequality of Opportunities" factor includes variables that reflect deprivation of those opportunities that are mainly related to young people's education, including quality of primary education and attainment. These four factors are expected to influence the four dimensions of urban inclusiveness.

1.3 The Basic Dynamics of Youth inequalities

1.3.1 Predetermined Circumstances

Urban poverty and inequality are inseparable from social exclusion processes. Social exclusion denies certain groups equal access to resources (economic, cultural and political) and prevents them from enjoying the same opportunities as other groups to improve their living standards. Growing numbers of young urban residents are bypassed by key political, social and economic processes. On occasion these young residents express their sense of frustration in ways that undermine urban cohesion and stability. Inequality features a number of intergenerational characteristics that are "passed on" across generations, depending on the extent to which the negative consequences of predetermined circumstances and issues like resources race or ethnicity, region of birth and parental education are circumscribed.

BOX 1.2 EDUCATION AND GENDER INEQUALITY

Over the past few decades, many developing countries have dramatically reduced gender gaps in primary and secondary education, as well as in literacy rates. UNESCO defines literacy as "the ability to identify, understand, interpret, create, communicate and compute, using printed and written materials associated with varying contexts. Literacy involves a continuum of learning to enable an individual to achieve his or her goals, to develop his or her knowledge and potential, and to participate fully in the wider society."[7] Education is universally recognized as one of the best ways of enhancing women's status. In this regard, Millennium Development Goal target 3a calls on governments to "eliminate gender disparity in primary and secondary education preferably by 2005, and at all levels by 2015." Female education results not just in individual development of personal potential and abilities, but is also beneficial to a country as a whole.

This goes to show that education plays a determinant role in increased incomes, improved health and nutrition and overcoming some aspects of poverty. Regrettably, inequalities are also generational, as children of poor parents tend to have unequal access to education, health and incomes.[8] A study conducted in Ecuador showed that maternal education had far-reaching effects on the next generation. Similarly, another United Nations report found that the probability of children's enrolment in schools increased as a function of mother's educational level.[9]

Figure 1.1 displays the Global Gender Gap Index as it stood in 2008 across the world's regions. Despite its achievements so far, sub-Saharan Africa is still rated last for gender equality in education.

FIGURE 1.2: **GLOBAL GENDER GAP INDEX**

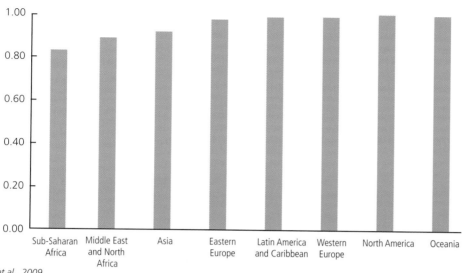

Source: Hausmann et.al., 2009

1.3.2 Family Resources and Location

Childhood residence and availability of resources to access basic services are also expected to influence the four types of inequality, although the impact could be more visible on economic, social and cultural inequalities. Lack of basic facilities could have adverse effects on the physical and mental growth of a child, which in turn could result in inability to access social, economic and cultural networks. Thus, respondents who spent their childhoods in more favourable locations with access to basic facilities are expected to feel more integrated with the rest of society.

De Barros *et. al.*[10] have assessed the degrees of inequality of opportunity in Latin America and the Caribbean using two techniques: (1) the Human Opportunity Index, to measure differences in opportunity among children; and (2) estimates of the share of current outcome inequalities that can be accounted for by circumstances that are beyond an individual's control. The first technique enables the authors to take the inequality debate a step further, focusing on inequality of opportunities for children rather than inequality of outcomes for adults. The issue here is not about equality, which de Barros et al. construct as equal rewards – i.e., equal chances for all.[11] The authors' major concern is for the influence of personal circumstances on children's access to the basic services that are necessary for a productive life. Basic services in this case include:

- access to water, sanitation and electricity

- completion of sixth grade at school (a proxy for access to basic education)

- school attendance at ages 10-14 (a proxy for access to late primary and early secondary education).

The authors consider these indicators as a subset of goods and services available to children and, therefore, as significant factors behind their economic advancement in life.

What, then, is the influence of personal circumstances – parents' education, family per capita income, gender, family structure (number of siblings, single-parent households and area of residence (urban vs. rural) – on access to basic services? To answer this question, experts have devised a human opportunity index for each of the 19 largest Latin American countries, based on data from nationally representative household surveys that represent 200 million children and range between 1995 and 2005.[12] This provides an overall picture of the degree of (in)equality prevailing in any given society.

1.3.3 Intergenerational inequalities

An important premise, when exploring inclusion and equity, is that opportunity deprivation and inequity affect a young person's status across different though interconnected spheres of urban activity and through successive life stages. Unequal access often begins in childhood and continues into youth and adulthood, consolidating any disadvantages faced in early years. By way of illustration, disadvantage in one sphere (like access to education) can lead to disadvantage in another – for instance, employment and housing.

Disadvantage can also increase exposure to the risk factors that undermine young people's development into responsible and productive adults. High degrees of inequity do contribute to higher levels of crime and weaker social capital, reflecting distrust between individuals and communities as well as social and political conflict.[13] The nurturing and protection of young people through equal access to shelter, education and services during childhood and the transition to adulthood is a capital investment that cannot be spared if stable and cohesive societies are to prevail.

Findings in Latin America suggest that "intergenerational transitions" accentuate any unequal status among children.[14] Research in Chile and Colombia showed that mother's education and father's income exert particularly powerful influence on the trend of their offspring's income levels in adulthood. However, the children's odds against future prosperity can be evened out by policy.

In this Report, intergenerational inequalities are measured in terms of levels of parents' education and earnings. It is expected that these will have some impact on the overall development of a child and her/his feeling of social inclusion. Parents who have benefited from higher education appreciate the related benefits and are more likely to invest in their offspring's knowledge and abilities, counting on the returns of the next generation's professional, economic and social advancement. Similarly, better-off parents can usually afford better quality education for their offspring. Therefore, one can expect that respondents whose parents are more educated and belong in relatively higher income brackets would give favourable responses regarding equality of opportunities.

Childhood residence influences various types of inequality
© **Mauricio Hora**

1.3.4 Inequality of Opportunities

The equal opportunity approach suggests a shift of emphasis in development policies and interventions from *outcomes* to *opportunities*. The onus lies largely on individual and community choices, efforts and talents to achieve the best possible outcomes. Equality of opportunity requires a leveling of the playing field, so that circumstances that are beyond an individual's control do not influence her/his life chances. Therefore, it is for policies and related schemes to break intergenerational inequality and improve outcomes for the new generations. If equality of opportunity is denied, the wealth of talent that is distributed across various social and economic segments remains untapped and is not mobilized for the benefit of society as a whole.

This Report makes many references to de Barros et al.[15] because theirs is the most recent empirical research, though limited to Latin America and the Carribean. These authors offer an empirical application of the equal opportunity approach, confirming its relevance in several ways. The methodological tools developed to test the equal opportunity approach has enabled them to demonstrate that in many instances, income inequality in adulthood is due to early, childhood circumstances over which individuals have no control. Adult access to, and use of, opportunity is therefore tainted by those accessed in childhood through parents.

Inequality of opportunities is the most important factor that is expected to influence outcome inequalities as it has a bi-directional relationship (see Figure 1.0). This is not the case with the other three factors. In this Report, inequality of opportunities is measured by the quality and levels of respondents' education. While young people are unlikely to be able to influence or determine the quality of primary education, they can improve their abilities as they grow up. If young people have access to better economic opportunities and activities, they can improve their levels of education, paving the way for their own economic, social and cultural advancement, as well as their integration in the social mainstream. This is why this Report is predicated on a bi-directional relationship between "Inequality of Opportunities" and "Outcome Inequalities".

1.4 Inequality of Opportunity acts as a drag on Growth and Development

There is no strong relationship between inequality and growth in rich countries. In addition, developing countries featuring high degrees of inequality tend to grow more slowly.

What is sometimes referred to as "destructive inequality" has been shown to be growth-inhibiting – and growth is what relatively poor countries require the most. In other words, economic growth finds itself hindered by inequality of opportunity and limited social mobility in a particular setting. Since there are no internationally comparable measures of opportunity or mobility, inequality (to the extent that inequality is growth-inhibiting) can be assumed to be of a of destructive nature.

Inequality matters because developing countries are not developed. According to Birdsall,[16] inequality matters most in developing countries because, by the very nature of being "developing" they are characterized by relatively weak markets and comparatively less effective governments when it comes to compensating for these weaknesses through public policy. The weakest link in societies, as with most systems, tends to act as a rate-determinant for the rest of that society – and developing countries are dominated by low value-adding, informal activities and low-skilled workforces that are increasingly made up of unemployed youth.

To summarize, the empirical relationship between income inequality and economic growth in developing countries suggests that:

- inequality involves a significant "destructive" component that is associated with unequal opportunities; and

- this "destructive" inequality contributes to lower growth.[17]

These findings are consistent with those of other scholars who have argued that inequality is inefficient from an economic perspective. As stressed by Sen,[18] "primitiveness of social development (such as widespread illiteracy, malnutrition, lack of health facilities and medical networks) is a barrier to the full realization of the benefits of participatory growth from which East Asia and Japan have profited". Against this background, concerns over equality should stand at the forefront of the development agenda.

1.5 Focus on Urban Youth

The focus of this Report on urban youth derives from two objective facts:

i.   statistics point to higher numbers of young people in the world today than ever before, and

ii. most are living in urban settlements.

Urban populations have undergone sustained expansion and the majority of their younger segments, particularly in developing countries, are coming of age and into adulthood in the poorest urban districts, i.e., slums. This unprecedented reality poses the twin challenges of urban opportunity and capacity development for the up-and-coming generations, if they are to contribute to the development of productive, resilient and sustainable cities for the sake of their own and their children's future. In order to meet this twin challenge, inequities in the urban population must be identified and their dynamics understood to inform appropriate, efficient policies. The "reimagining" of urban society and the way it supports present and future generations is an urgent task.

Projections suggest that nearly all of the demographic expansion of the next 30 years will be concentrated in urban areas.[19] By 2020, at least 52 per cent of the population in developing countries will live in cities. The bulk of this growth is likely to take place in Asia and Africa. Asia will be host to 15 of the world's 27 "mega-cities" by 2015 (i.e., those with populations over 10 million). By 2030, an estimated 60 per cent of the world population will live in cities, and a similar proportion of these urban residents will be under 18.[20] Today, more than 70 per cent of Africa's urban population lives in slums. The majority of these urban slum dwellers are young (as defined by the United Nations, i.e., aged between 15 and 24).

As the first decade of the 21st century is about to come to a close, almost half of the world's population is under 24, of which 1.2 billion are younger than 15. While the overall share of children and youth in the global population is shrinking as fertility rates decline, in absolute numbers there are more young people today than ever before. Almost 85 per cent of young people live in developing countries, and 60 per cent are in Asia.[21] In developing regions as a whole, least-developed countries are younger than the rest of the world: in 2005, the global median age was 28 years, but in 10 least-developed African countries it was 16 or younger.[22]

Even though today's youth are reckoned to be the best educated and healthiest in history,[23] their vulnerability to unemployment and disease remains significant. According to the International Labour Organization (ILO), young people are more likely to be unemployed than the adult working population.[24] UNESCO[25] states that one-third of the 20 million in the world who have died of HIV/AIDS-related conditions were young people; and another 6,000 are infected every day. Youth are also dying of respiratory infections and preventable diseases and malnutrition. Drug dependency, suicide and violence are putting millions of urban youth "at risk" across all regions.

Urban youth include all those living in cities and townships under local government administration.[26] The diversity among them is as great as in any other social group. Some are educated and articulate, having had access to the best opportunities that modern amenities and education can provide; but the majority of urban youth in the developing regions are underprivileged. The UN Department of Economic and Social Affairs (UN DESA) splits disadvantaged youth into 11 distinct categories, as follows:[27]

1. those without adequate access to education and health services;

2. adolescents who have dropped out of school;

3. pregnant adolescents, whether married or not;

4. married adolescents;

5. young single parents;

6. young people who are HIV-positive, or at particular risk of HIV/AIDS;

7. young refugees or displaced persons;

8. racial, linguistic and ethnic minorities;

9. homeless youth;

10. young people with disabilities; and

11. girls and young women in any of these groups that are affected by gender inequalities.

Since youth is a transitional period, one of identity building and the "springboard" for an individual's definition as an adult, disadvantage and deprivation at this stage are likely to continue into adulthood.

1.6 Youth Mobility and Vulnerability

This transition period is one of high mobility for young people as they look for work in cities. Many move from rural to urban areas and within cities in search of opportunities to gain skills and income. In 2007 the World Bank[28] stated that in the 29 developing countries with data, youth are 40 per cent more likely than older generations to move from rural to urban areas or simply across urban areas.

Migration rates tend to peak, for both males and females, between ages 15 to 24[29] as young people take risks and move away from families and friends in search of jobs. In India, urban in-migration of informal and self-employed workers soared by an estimated 360 per cent in the 1990s.[30] Young people make significant contributions to these flows of migrants from rural areas. Their loneliness and disorientation make them particularly vulnerable to exploitation. Like its equivalent for children, youth protection does not feature in most urban agendas.

"At risk" youth in urban settings include all those girls and boys whose living or health conditions, circumstances or behaviour patterns place them at risk of falling victims to, or being involved in, crime. They include, but are not limited to, youth already at odds with the law, those living in urban slums, street children, youth gangs, school drop-outs, unemployed youth, substance-abusing youth, those who are sexually exploited, war-affected children, and those affected by the AIDS pandemic including orphans. These groups include both girls and boys. Girls in particular are often targets of sexual exploitation, and are therefore particularly vulnerable to HIV/AIDS infection.

Youth caught in worsening situations of inequality and impoverishment are excluded from opportunities for socialization under adult responsibility norms. A UNDP report on Youth and Conflict describes this condition as "youth crisis", which means that the transition from childhood to adulthood is "blocked."[31] The report states that full adulthood is increasingly difficult to achieve due to social and economic constraints.

For example, millions of African youth living in deplorable conditions and without access to predictable routes to jobs, marriage and the setting up of households, are caught "in limbo", as described below :

For many young Africans, "youth" is not serving as a *transitional phase to a more established social status, but is an enduring limbo. This is a source of tremendous frustration. Instead of leaving youth behind and entering adulthood by marrying and establishing independent households, an increasing proportion of this "lost generation"... are unable to attain any social status.*[32]

In such situations, being a "gangster" or "militia" confers on a young person a status of sorts. However, once war or conflict ends, these same youth are no longer given the recognition they had, and this marginalization can further exacerbate their involvement in violent behaviour and crime.

Young people need to be protected from negative influences that can derail the transition into healthy adulthood. Targeted and special attention can mitigate risk factors, but it is a short timespan (between adolescence and young adulthood) within which this change can be made. If youth development is left unaddressed by government and other stakeholders, young people's vulnerability to engage in crime and conflict situations can increase. At the same time, it is important to recognize that millions of young people are not engaged in negative social behaviour. To ensure that this remains, targeted strategies are needed. This is well recognized in this observation from Brazil:[33]

In general, programmes treat what is conventionally called the "at-risk group" in a uniform manner, without employing specific strategies. It is commonly thought that programmes for young people in "areas" considered to be of higher risk, will reach all at-risk youths. However, this ignores the fact that it is a diverse group, and that it is therefore necessary to create specific and focused strategies. It is important to highlight the fact that young people who live in "high-risk" areas, due to the higher levels of violence there, should not automatically be classed as "at-risk groups", since the majority of them are not involved in any type of criminal or illegal activity.

Policies and strategies that enhance equal opportunity for young people and put them at the centre of development, are required to counter negative situations and intercept intergenerational transfer of risk, disadvantage and marginalization. This will pave the way for a proper transition into adulthood, one that enables young people to take advantage of opportunities to develop their potential and make their own contributions to society.

Successful transition is usually marked by productive presence in the labour market and participation in civic and electoral processes. However, this transition is becoming almost an impossible dream for millions living in substandard and crowded accommodation (if any at all, as homeless youth are a prevailing phenomenon across all regions). Young people tend to have very limited access to basic infrastructure, with exposure to frequent disease outbreaks in urban slums, and are caught in an under/un/employment trap. At present and as mentioned earlier, 60 per cent of the world's slum dwellers live in Asia. More than 70 per cent of the African urban population lives in slums. The majority of these urban slum dwellers are young people.

1.7 UN-HABITAT's Survey of Urban Youth Inequality

This Report investigates young peoples' perceptions of urban inclusiveness and equality of opportunity in five cities in sub-Saharan Africa, Asia, Latin America and the Caribbean. These four regions feature varying degrees of urbanization and inequality; but the selected cities are representative insofar as they are all host to ever-growing numbers of unemployed young people and are on trend to become "mega" cities.

The United Nations definition of youth as individuals between the ages of 15 and 24 is not legally binding. The Convention on the Rights of the Child defines a "child" as anyone under the age of 18. National definitions of youth vary and can range from 12 to 35 years of age.

Of equal importance as the age categories are social perceptions of the moment when a youth makes the transition into adulthood, and of the degree of responsibility expected of them. Cultural expectations and traditions have a bearing on the point when youth can be expected to take on decisionmaking roles, or be "heard" as serious contributors to social, political and economic decisions. This affects their roles in local governance and economic decisionmaking.

These different criteria suggest that national and local contexts must be taken into account when identifying the "young" segment of any population. Common across all definitions is a consensus that youth is the period of transition from school to work and from childhood to adulthood. It is a very distinct stage between childhood and adulthood. This is also when an individual looks to move from dependence to independence.

Too many youths are neither at school nor at work. Colombo, Sri Lanka
© Suzi Mutter

1.8 The Basic Characteristics of Young Survey Respondents

For the purposes of the survey at the core of this Report, UN-HABITAT distributed questionnaires to a total 729 young people in the five selected cities (Kingston, Lagos, Mumbai, Nairobi and Rio de Janeiro), and focus group meetings were held in each city to discuss the issues. The respondents' distribution by city and gender is described in Figures 1.2 and 1.3. The sampling is purposive, i.e., subjectively chosen by survey coordinators, and is not similar across the five cities. Still, there are remarkable similarities in some of the findings in terms of youth perceptions of equity and intergenerational transfer of inequality.

The city-wise distribution of respondents by gender is presented in Figure 1.3. The figure shows that the highest proportion (54.29 per cent) of female respondents were in Kingston and the lowest (32.26 per cent) in Lagos. The proportion of female respondents in Mumbai was 35.12 per cent. On the other hand, the proportions of female respondents in Nairobi and Rio de Janeiro were 45.35 and 52.53 per cent respectively. Only two cities had more than 50 per cent female respondents, namely, Kingston and Rio de Janeiro.

FIGURE 1.3: **DISTRIBUTION OF RESPONDENTS BY CITY AND GENDER**

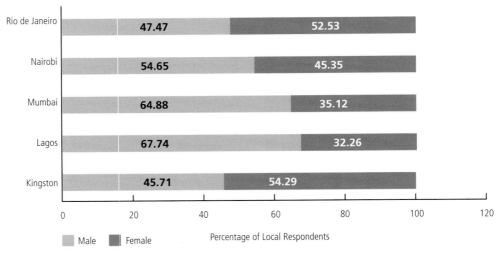

Source: UN-HABITAT, 2009

FIGURE 1.4: **DISTRIBUTION OF RESPONDENTS BY CITY AND LEVEL OF EDUCATION**

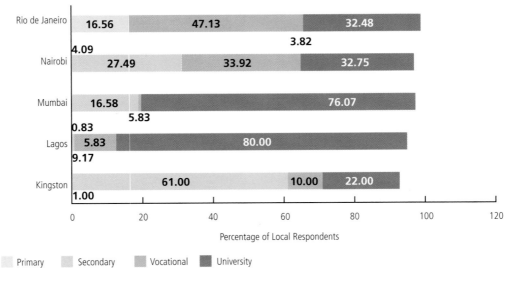

Source: UN-HABITAT, 2009

The highest or the second highest percentages of respondents in the five cities had university education. More than 50 per cent of respondents had completed secondary or higher education.

This Report assesses youth perceptions of inclusiveness and equality of opportunity in four major spheres of urban life – political, social, economic and cultural. Inclusiveness is assessed against these four parameters, which are taken to be synonomous with increased equity.

In order to supplement subjective interview data and provide a more robust interpretation of the survey in the five cities, national data is used to identify the functional forms of relationship between inequality of opportunities and outcome inequalities.

1.9 The Structure of the Report

Chapter 1 introduces the Report and presents the major factors behind inequality of opportunity. Chapter 2 examines education of both young people and parents as a critical driver of opportunity equality. Chapter 3 reviews family resources and location inequality. This includes the major findings of the survey with regard to education, employment and access to basic services. Chapter 4 discusses young people's perceptions of their "right to the city" based on the surveys and the focus group discussions in the five selected cities. Chapter 5 offers some policy recommendations for the promotion of equal opportunities for young people.

BOX 1.3 THE MACROECONOMIC ANALYSIS OF INEQUALITY

The seven variables representing various inequalities included in the analysis are the following: Gini coefficients (i.e., measures of income/consumption inequality across a given population), per capita health expenditure, maternal mortality rate, percentage of population with access to improved sanitation and safe drinking water, per capita GDP, female enrolment ratio in secondary education, and enrolment ratio in primary, secondary and tertiary education.

Gini coefficients are treated as proxies for outcome inequality, The various enrolment ratios have been taken as representative of inequality of opportunities. In addition, maternal mortality rates and other variables (such as expenditure on health and access to improved infrastructure) represent location-specific inequalities. Typically, while people living in slums do have access to such facilities, they are poorly supplied, while those living in gated communities tend to have access to better facilities.

Data have been collected from World Development Indicators.[33] The Gini coefficient measures the area between the Lorenz curve and a hypothetical line of absolute equality, expressed as a percentage of the maximum area under the line. Therefore, a Gini coefficient of 0 represents perfect equality, while a 100 value implies perfect inequality. Per capita expenditure is expressed in US dollars at current prices, with subsequent conversion to purchasing power parity for the sake of comparability (based on the ratio of GDP per capita at constant 2005 prices to GDP per capita at current prices). Maternal mortality is measured as the average of deaths per 1,000 births. Enrolment ratios are in percentage terms, while sanitation and water-related variables were measured as percentages of populations supplied with improved sanitation facilities and access to safe drinking water. Per capita GDP in US dollars was measured at constant 2005 prices.

Any association of macroeconomic variables typically opens up a debate over the direction of causality. In order to anticipate on criticisms, a simultaneous rather than single equation model has been used in this Report. Lagged variables have been used to reflect the time it takes for capital investment to have an influence on national variables. For instance, enrolment ratios in primary, secondary and tertiary education may affect GDP only after a number of years. With these relationships in mind, data for 1990 and 2005 have been collected for all the variables, except enrolment in tertiary education for which 1991 figures have been used. Figures for access to sanitation and water variables for 2005 were interpolated from 2000 and 2006 data.

END NOTES

[1] Birdsall, 2005.
[2] Roemer, 1998.
[3] Sen, 1976; Roemer, 2006; de Barros et. al., 2009.
[4] De Barros et al., op. cit.
[5] UN-HABITAT, 2010a.
[6] De Barros et al., 2009.
[7] UNESCO, 2009.
[8] World Bank, 2006.
[9] De Barros et al., 2009.
[10] Ibid.
[11] Ibid.
[12] UN-HABITAT, 2005.
[13] UN 2002.
[14] Ibid.
[15] Ibid.

[16] Birdsall, 2005.
[17] Ibid.
[18] Sen, 1999.
[19] UN-HABITAT 2010a, Ch. 1.1.
[20] UNDP, 2006.
[21] UNESCO, 2004.
[22] UN-HABITAT, 2006.
[23] World Bank, 2007.
[24] ILO, 2009.
[25] UNESCO, 2004:5.
[26] "Urban" is usually defined as settlements with populations of 150,000 or more, governed under city or municipal status with an elected mayor. However, this definition is subject to variation depending on country size and

level of development.
[27] UN DESA, 2005.
[28] World Bank, 2007.
[29] UN DESA, 2005.
[30] Satyanayana, 2009.
[31] UNDP, 2006.
[32] Spinks, 2002.
[33] Viva Rio, 2005.
[33] World Bank staff estimates based on primary household survey data obtained from government statistical agencies and World Bank country departments. For more information and methodology, please see PovcalNet (http://iresearch.worldbank.org/PovcalNet/jsp/index.jsp).

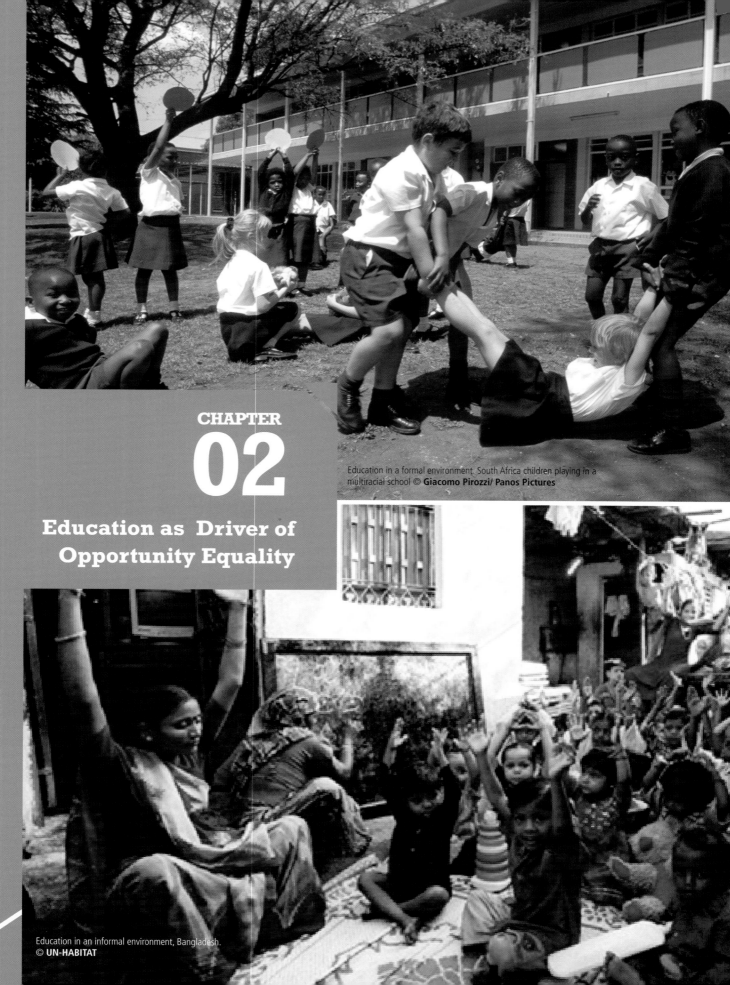

CHAPTER

02

Education as Driver of Opportunity Equality

Education in a formal environment. South Africa children playing in a multiracial school © **Giacomo Pirozzi/ Panos Pictures**

Education in an informal environment, Bangladesh.
© **UN-HABITAT**

> ## "Education is our greatest opportunity to give an irrevocable gift to the next generation."
> Ernie Fletcher

2.0 Introduction

An emerging literature on the role of education and human well-being shows that access to schooling, as measured in large part by enrolment and completion rates, drives much of the observed inequality of outcomes. The correlation between basic education, economic growth and industrialization is a strong one. Schooling, according to human capital theory, is a capital investment that directly enhances workers' productivity.[1] The current "youth bulge" – the largest number of young people the world has ever seen – presents an unprecedented opportunity to put young people's creativity and talent to good use for the sake of economic growth and social enhancement, especially as today's youth are the healthiest and most educated in history.[2] If we are to make the most of this favourable demographic situation, which is typical of developing regions today, we must provide formal and non-formal learning platforms to generate skilled human capital that can drive productivity growth and social innovation.

Beyond building human capital to raise worker productivity, another instrumental function of education is to provide young individuals with what they need to become effective agents of change (as detailed in Chapter 4). This will be achieved in part by improving the quality of education and access to all essential services, as well as optimizing opportunities for access to and accumulation of assets. Providing young people with the necessary capabilities and learning opportunities can enhance their "authentic engagement" in decisions that affect them.[3] The potential for enhanced growth through a "demographic dividend" lies in the potential productivity of a larger, skilled labour supply, as well as lower degrees of dependency and greater ability to save and invest. Instead of this, a majority of young people in the developing world do not receive the requisite education and live in environments characterized by squalor and poverty, which hinders the potential and energy they otherwise could have contributed to the common good.

Inclusion and equality of opportunity are the foundations upon which young people tend to develop their abilities for "agency", i.e., their ability to shape the world. The development of identity and agency as a social process is a close function of individuals' opportunities for quality education and skills. Lave[4] confirmed that to craft an identity is "a social process, and to be more knowledgeable is an aspect of participation in social practice." As they form their identities, adolescents and young adults sense a desire to exert more agency in shaping their world. Whether urban systems are able to offer them equal opportunities for this depends on the understanding of those who craft these systems. Youth capacity to exert agency is, to a considerable extent, shaped by the education and training they receive.

The specification of the econometric model behind the findings in this Report is based on the assumption that higher GDP leads to reductions in income inequality. Income disparity is also influenced by the proportion of educated youth in a given population. It is also assumed that female educational achievement affects income inequality, too. This Report assumes that the overall educational attainment of a given population affects per capita GDP with a lag of some years, and higher per capita GDP is expected to lead to smaller income disparities. This association is captured in Figure 2.1, where the 2005 Gini coefficient of income inequality has been plotted against enrolment in primary and secondary education in 1990, and enrolment in tertiary education in 1991.

In Figure 2.1, the slopes of trend lines for the three indicators of education are negative, suggesting that the higher the enrolment ratio in 1990, the lower income inequality was in 2005. The association confirms our assumption that past investment in education results in lower income inequalities in the future. In other words, failure to invest in the education of youth increases the risk and incidence of future inequalities, and the consequences that come with them.

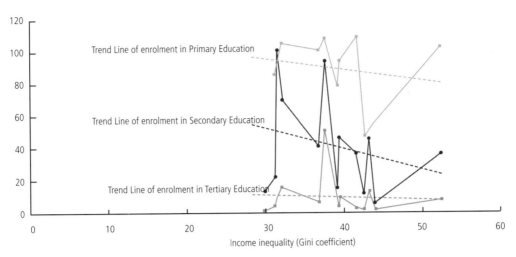

Source: UN-HABITAT, 2009

This association between enrolment in secondary education and income inequality is depicted in Figure 2.1, with particular regard to the relationship between income inequality and female education. Female enrolment in secondary education is used as a proxy for female education in general. The relationship between Gini coefficients and female enrolment in secondary education is depicted in Figure 2.2.

The negative slope of the trend line shown in Figure 2.2 suggests that the association of female enrolment in secondary education with income inequality follows the same pattern as that of total enrolment in secondary education. In other words, capital investment in female youth education helps shape the future as it reduces inequality.

FIGURE 2.2: **INCOME INEQUALITY AND FEMALE ENROLMENT IN SECONDARY EDUCATION**

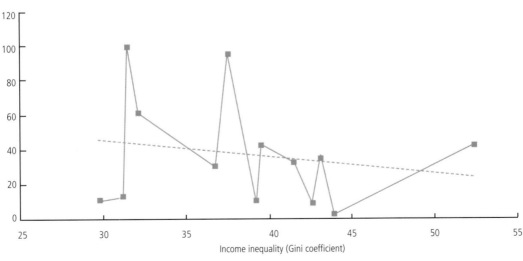

Source: UN-HABITAT, 2009

2.1 Characterizing Education Opportunity in the Five Cities

Figure 2.3 compares and ranks the various sources and nature of opportunity deprivation of various categories of urban dwellers. In the five cities under review, more than 60 per cent of young males and females ranked "uneducated people" as deprived of opportunities. The lowest proportion (59.73 per cent) of such respondents was found in Mumbai and the highest (92.90 per cent) in Rio de Janeiro.

Equally, slum dwellers, who are usually poor and sometimes illiterate, are identified as "highly deprived" of opportunities in the five cities, with the highest proportion (92.26 per cent) in Rio de Janeiro. The other two categories of people that are considered opportunity-deprived are the elderly and the disabled. The highest proportion (80 per cent) of respondents was in Lagos, where disabled people were categorized as "deprived".

FIGURE 2.3: **PERCEIVED DEPRIVATION OF OPPORTUNITY – BY CATEGORY AND CITY (% OF LOCAL RESPONDENTS)**

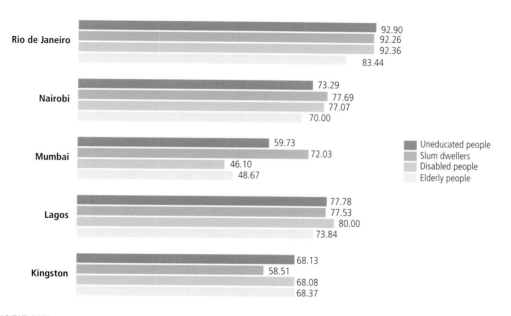

Source: UN-HABITAT, 2009

To a significant extent, inequality is determined by the quality of education. Inequality of educational opportunity occurs when the quality of education is determined by child's class, race or social status. As will be detailed in Chapter 3, a wide set of family resource factors such as location of home (slum or non-slum), total income and father's income contribute to increased social inequality. Schooling and those institutions regulating access to enrolment somehow contribute to the urban class and race divide. When educational allocation is driven by unequal and asymmetric political decisionmaking structures, youth from poorer backgrounds tend to bear the brunt of policies. Significantly, children from slums and poor backgrounds have tended to rate poorly in test scores and have low college enrolment rates.

Based on the UN-HABITAT 2009 Urban Youth Survey, Figure 2.4 depicts young respondents' rankings of primary education. The quality of locally available primary education is perceived as only "average" by a majority of respondents with average quality of education in four cities: Kingston (37.14 per cent), Mumbai (47.31 per cent), Nairobi (53.57 per cent) and Rio de Janeiro (49.04 per cent). Lagos featured the highest proportion (46.34 per cent) of respondents with high-quality primary education. On average, 46.34 per cent of the respondents described the quality of local primary education as "high".

FIGURE 2.4: **PERCEIVED QUALITY OF LOCAL PRIMARY EDUCATION – RANKING BY CITY**

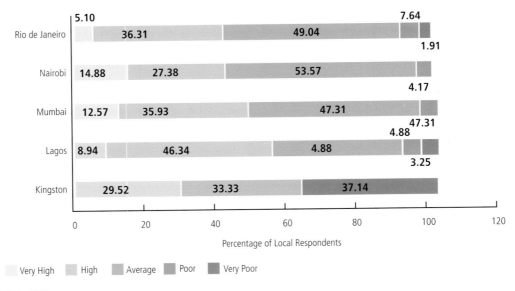

Source: UN-HABITAT , 2009

2.2 Education Inequality as the Root of Multiple Deprivations

The main objective ot the UN-HABITAT 2009 Urban Youth Survey was to assess how young people perceived the degree of inclusiveness of their cities under four dimensions of equality: social, economic, cultural and political. The results appear in Figure 2.5.

FIGURE 2.5: **PERCEPTIONS OF INCLUSIVENESS BY LEVEL OF EDUCATION – FIVE CITIES**

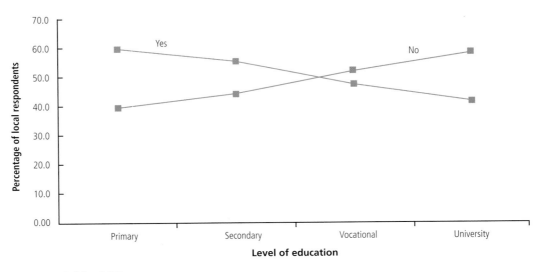

Note: Chi-square: 18.718; Level of Sig.: 0.096
Source: UN-HABITAT, 2009

The association between inequality of education levels and the perceived degree of non-inclusiveness is clear in Figure 2.5. The proportion of young people who said their city denied them equal opportunities was significantly higher among those with primary education only (60 per cent) than among those with university education (41.6 per cent). This shows that the more educated respondents tend to have better social, political, cultural and income opportunities in their respective cities compared with those less educated. The association between the level of education and urban opportunity and inclusiveness is statistically significant at the 10 per cent level. This finding corroborates the fact that the better educated people are able to access opportunities more easily than those less educated.

Research show as clear evidence that the unequal distribution of college students' enrolment is related to an individual's socio-economic background, as demonstrated by comparisons between college enrolment rates and demographics. One study analysed the top 146 colleges in the United States of America[5] and found the following pattern: 75 per cent of students were from socioeconomic backgrounds consistent with the richest 25 per cent of the population, and fewer than 5 per cent were from the poorest 25 per cent of the population. Clearly, the notion of social mobility, with youth moving seamlessly from rags to riches if only they work hard, is no more than a myth, as long as the playing field is not levelled.

The focus now turns to the relationship between youth with primary education only, on the one hand, and employment prospects, on the other – employment being a strong pointer to social inclusion. The average proportion of respondents ranking the quality of primary education and employment prospects in their city as "average" is 45.83 per cent, compared with 35.42 per cent who rank it as "high".

The analysis suggests that Kingston has the highest proportion (29.52 per cent) of youth with "very high" quality of primary education, and Rio de Janeiro has the lowest (5.10 per cent); these are subjective answers from the youth focus group discussions. On the other hand, Lagos features the highest proportion of young people with "high" quality of primary education (46.34 per cent), and Nairobi the lowest (27.38 per cent). The Kenyan capital is where the proportion of respondents with "average" quality of education is the highest (53.57 per cent), and Lagos where it is the lowest (36.59 per cent). Overall, 45.83 per cent of sample respondents said the quality of primary education in their city was only "average", and 35.42 per cent found it "high".

2.3 Parents' Education and Intergenerational Inequality

A comparative assessment of inequality of opportunity in educational achievement based on predetermined circumstances and others that include individual efforts, talent and good fortune has been carried out in five Latin American and nine North American and European countries.[6] It showed that as is the case with inequality of economic opportunity, family background variables (and particularly mother's education and father's occupation) are the most significant determinants of inequality in educational achievement. School location is an important variable in Mexico. Gender was found to have only a limited effect on unequal educational achievement.

By comparison with the Organisation for Economic Co-operation and Development (OECD) area, educational achievement is more unequal in Latin American countries. Where the proportion of total inequality due to predetermined circumstances is only 15 per cent in OECD countries, it stands at 20 per cent in Latin America. Opportunity profiles for the least and most advantaged in educational achievement reveal that for all countries, the least advantaged groups feature parents who are agricultural workers with little or no schooling. In Chile and Mexico, those most disadvantaged in terms of education have been to school in rural areas, but the opposite holds in Argentina and Brazil where they are predominantly found in urban areas. Gender plays a role here: boys are the most disadvantaged in the "reading category", while girls dominate in both reading and mathematics.

To summarize, parental background variables play a significant role in intergenerational inequality. These variables appear to shape the opportunities available to their offspring and are most influential on groups at the bottom of both the economic and educational ladders. Figure 2.6 shows the city-wise distribution of youth by the educational level of their fathers.

Figure 2.6 shows that three cities feature the highest proportions of respondents whose fathers had university education: Lagos (49.11 per cent), Mumbai (36.09 per cent) and Nairobi (40.99 per cent). Kingston features the highest proportion (42.86 per cent) of respondents whose fathers had secondary education only, and Rio de Janeiro is where the proportion of respondents whose fathers had primary education only was the highest (32 per cent).

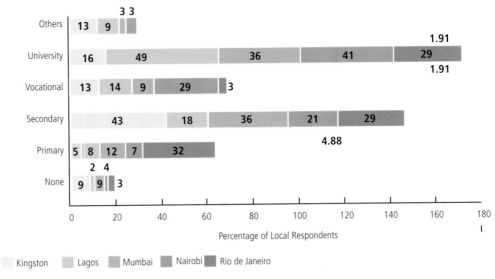

Source: UN-HABITAT , 2009

2.4 The Influence of Education on Outcome Opportunities

In the five cities, more than 50 per cent of respondents had fathers without university or secondary education.

The distribution of youths by their mothers' level of education is depicted in Figure 2.7, and is similar to that of the fathers'. These results are not surprising, as it is very common in large cities to have parents with largely similar levels of education.

The UN-HABITAT Urban Youth Survey 2009 confirms the strong effect of education on various aspects of economic and political opportunities for urban youth inclusion. The deprivation of economic opportunity depicted in Table 2.1 shows that the educational opportunities availed to both the young people and their parents have a direct effect on their economic opportunities. Parents' educational level is significant at 1 per cent while respondents' education is significant at 5 per cent.

FIGURE 2.7: **MOTHER'S EDUCATION – DISTRIBUTION BY CITY**

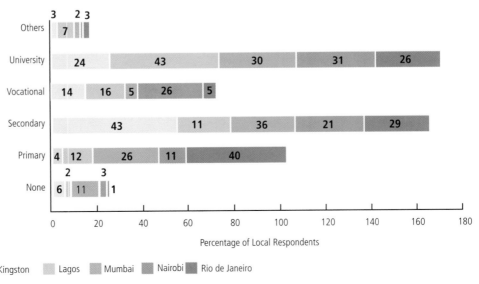

Source: UN-HABITAT Survey, 2009

The substantial intergenerational influence on young people's economic opportunities is quite clear. A majority of those with higher educational levels found that economic opportunities were not equitably distributed in their respective cities. If this group have this perception, then the more educationally disadvantaged respondents will have an even stronger one.

The statistically strong significance in the opinion of those young respondents whose parents are more educated shows the non-negligible impact of the educational level of parents and how this, in turn, affects the educational attainment of their offspring. Education changes not just individuals' perceptions of society, but also provides them with the instrumental capabilities to shape society; in other words, education is both the means as well as the end of development.[7]

A UN-HABITAT study on gender disparity in literacy[8] shows a strong positive association between the literacy rates of both genders but is negatively correlated with male-headed households. A multivariate analysis shows the association between female heads of households and literacy rates. Although the value of R^2 of the trend lines is not very high, the coefficient is positive, showing that mother's education promotes child literacy.

The polynomial of girls' enrolment rate (Fig. 2.8) is higher than that of boys when examined by levels of education (primary and secondary), the quantified relationship between household head, gender and enrolment at the primary school level. This suggests a strong relationship between girls' primary education and mother's education in urban areas.

The effect of education on inequality of political opportunities is just as powerful. Of all the different proxy measures, three variables in Table 2.1 – namely, "exclusion based on caste and creed", "access to basic services" and "quality of primary education" – significantly influence the propensity to political opportunity. In this particular dimension, the "Intergenerational Inequalities" factor does not significantly influence respondents' perceptions. As might have been expected, the more highly educated participants in the survey do not agree with the opinion that the "city does not protect human rights at all". Again, those youth with early, privileged access to basic services also tend to be those who had access to better quality of primary education. They are the best placed for access to political office, and therefore take advantage of networks and class to make the most of the political opportunities that come their way.

FIGURE 2.8: **FEMALE HEADS OF HOUSEHOLDS AND LITERACY RATE (MOTHER'S EDUCATION)**

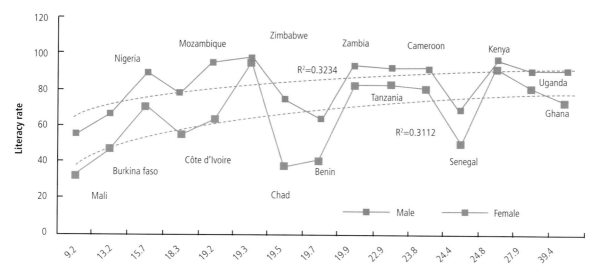

Source: UN-HABITAT, 2008b

VARIABLES	ECONOMIC OPPORTUNITY	MEAN	F-STATISTICS	POLITICAL OPPORTUNITY	MEAN	F-STATISTICS
SEX OF RESPONDENT	MALE (256)	1.43	0.94	MALE (557)	1.44	0.007
	FEMALE (462)	1.44	[.759]	FEMALE (153)	1.44	[.934]
EXCLUSION BASED ON CASTE AND CREED	YES (349)	3.02	0.632	YES (72)	2.49	5.066
			[.427]			[.025]
CHILDHOOD PLACE OF RESIDENCE	YES (448)	2.14	0.521	YES (152)	2.2	0.948
			[.471]			[.330]
ACCESS TO BASIC FACILITIES	YES (455)	1.2	0.012	YES (153)	1.12	.6.322
			[.913]			[.012]
QUALITY OF PRIMARY EDUCATION	YES (457)	2.46	0.574	YES(154)	2.19	18.702
			[.449]			[.000]
EDUCATION LEVEL OF RESPONDENTS	YES (456)	4.19	4.664	YES(151)	4.09	0.159
			[.031]			[.690]
EDUCATION LEVEL OF FATHER	YES (438)	3.64	7.392	YES (148)	3.78	0.039
			[.007]			[.844]
EDUCATION LEVEL OF MOTHER	YES (454)	3.64	7.337	YES (151)	3.46	0.8
			[.007]			[.371]
EMPLOYMENT OF FATHER	YES (408)	2.81	0.016	YES (91)	2.84	0.44
			[.900]			[.508]

Source: UN-HABITAT, 2009

Note: Figures in parenthesis are no. of respondents while in square brackets are level of significance

2.5 Income Inequality determines Enrolment, Attendance and Literacy

The availability of schools in urban areas is not a sufficient reason for children to be enrolled. Families in slum communities, in particular, often cannot afford to send their children to school because the combined costs of fees, textbooks and uniforms are prohibitive. In Kenya, for example, the government mandated free primary education in 2003, but it is still for students' parents to purchase uniforms and supplies and pay fees for examinations, which makes it difficult for low-income families to send their offspring to school and secure their advancement. Even in slum areas served by several schools, the number of these may still not be adequate, further hindering access to quality education. Research in the Nairobi slum of Kibera in 2003[9] found that, although as many as 14 public primary schools were located within walking distance, they could only accommodate a total of 20,000 students. This left out more than 100,000 slum children unable to attend school.

This situation is corroborated by research in the Gambia,[10] which shows that although fees for state primary education have been waived, school-related costs are estimated by official sources to consume 2.4 per cent of the average per capita income of the poorest quintile of Gambian households. In most cases, youth from poor households have to work to pay for their education. Poverty is closely related to school non-attendance and drop-out numbers.

According to Jones and Chant,[11] in Ghana young people have reported that they dropped out of school in order to earn enough to continue, in the process extending school attendance and training well into adulthood. In other words, income and economic opportunity lie behind the pattern of enrolment rates which, quite frequently, are not reflected in attendance or completion rates. Even among those who do attend school, the education many receive is of such poor standards that they leave without basic literacy or numeracy skills. In Ghana and Zambia, fewer than 60 per cent of all 15-19 year-olds who have completed six years of education are able to read a simple sentence in their own language.[12] In Ghana, state school attendees sometimes seek private tuition to help with literacy and numeracy.[13]

UNESCO's 2009 *Education For All (EFA) Global Monitoring Report* stresses[14] that for all the gains made in universal primary education (the average net enrolment ratios for developing countries have been on a steady increase since the year 2000), there is still a long way to go. For example, sub-Saharan Africa raised its average net enrolment ratio from 54 to 70 per cent between 1999 and 2006, a six-fold annual increase on preceding years. The increases in South and West Asia were also significant (from 75 to 86 per cent). In Latin America, the net enrolment ratio for primary school is 95 per cent, but a wide gap remains between rich and poor as well as between indigenous and non-indigenous populations.

Where are the women in the class? Hydraform Blockmaking Training – Kitui, Kenya.
© **UN-HABITAT**

The international focus on Millennium Development Goals (MDGs), for instance, has helped to direct resources to increase primary school enrolment. A significant number of children have benefited from this; for example, in India, more than half of young females aged 15-19 years have no primary education, but the younger generations are given the opportunity to attend primary school.[15]

A large proportion of Latin American youth (almost one third of 20-24 year-olds in 2002) have not completed primary education and the secondary school completion rates are worse. In Brazil, a country where 20 per cent of the population is between 15 and 24 years old, only about 55 per cent of 15 to 17 year-olds attend secondary school or university.[16]

To summarize, disparities based on wealth, gender, location, ethnicity and other markers for disadvantage also persist in terms of school attendance. While children from the wealthiest 20 per cent of households have already achieved universal primary school attendance in most countries, those from the poorest 20 per cent have not.

2.6 Gender Inequities Persist at Secondary and Tertiary levels

Although gender parity in enrolment at the primary level has improved, girls still made up 55 per cent of the 75 million children not at school in 2006.[17] The gender gap remains particularly prevalent at secondary and tertiary levels. In Southern Asia and Eastern Africa, more girls of secondary school age are likely to be out of school than in school.[18] In many sub-Saharan African countries, 40 to 60 per cent of women are married before the age of 18. The worldwide tertiary gender equality ratio was around 24 per cent in 2005, but it stood at only 5 per cent in sub-Saharan Africa and 11 per cent in Southern and Western Asia, compared with 70 per cent in North America and Western Europe.[19]

In sub-Saharan Africa, according to the *2007 World Youth Report*,[20] young women pursuing tertiary education are less likely to graduate in science or mathematics, although these are especially relevant in today's global economy. Few females graduate in engineering, manufacturing, construction, science or agriculture. This suggests that their opportunities in the professional world are influenced not only by their educational achievements, but also by the socio-cultural factors that influence the educational paths of boys and girls.

Young women's reproductive role is also an inhibiting factor in gender parity in education. Figure 2.9 shows comparative proportions of young women in urban slums and non-slums who dropped out of school due to early marriage or pregnancy.[21] In a majority of the countries, the proportions are higher in slums, which may reflect the compounded disadvantage slum-dwelling girls are facing.

UNESCO's 2009 EFA[22] report recognizes the disadvantage perpetuated by persistent inequalities and predetermined circumstances such as income, gender, location, ethnicity, language and physical disability, and stresses that greater attention is required from governments. Governments must act to reduce disparities through effective policy reforms and break down inequalities in education.

FIGURE 2.9 **FEMALE SCHOOL DROP-OUT RATE (PREGNANCY/EARLY MARRIAGE, 15-24) – SLUMS AND NON-SLUMS (%)**

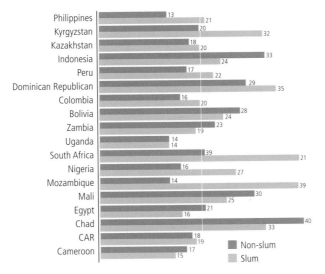

Source: UN-HABITAT, 2010b

2.7 Youth Underemployment Slows Development

In addition to widespread youth unemployment, under-employment of skills remains pervasive, which in a broad sense speaks of under-utilization of labour and, by extension, human capital. Youth under-employment results when relatively high-skilled workers are constrained to hold down low-earning jobs. For instance, recently graduated computer scientists and engineers are forced to work as shop attendants or drivers when proper employment avenues are closed to them. Young people are sometimes forced to take on part-time jobs and to this extent do not use their full capacities because full-time employment is unavailable. This category is sometimes referred to as "involuntary part-time workers".

At a critical juncture in their lives, just when they need to acquire skills and work experience, significant proportions of young people are neither at school nor at work in Latin America and the Caribbean, Africa and Asia. These are the "idle" youth who do not make it to secondary school and are neither employed nor self-employed. In Africa, 27 per cent of youth are neither in school nor at work, a situation that can lead to frustration, delinquency and social exclusion.[24] For example, in Kenya, 38 per cent (2 out of every 5) of young people are neither in school nor work.[25] Their vulnerability to incitement was apparent in Kenya's post-election chaos in 2008.

In Latin America in 2002, about 18 per cent of those between the ages of 15 and 19 were neither studying nor working, and about 27 per cent of those between 20 and 24 were in a similar situation.[26] Almost 25 per cent of young people aged between 18 and 24 in Rio's *favela* communities do not work or study, and 70 per cent are young women.[27] High rates of adolescent pregnancy may be related to ever-increasing non-occupation rates among urban youth as well as contributing to the high numbers of young women out of school or work. Unless non-formal training and further education are there to offer them a second chance, these young people may remain marginalized and idle.

Provision of employable and life skills must be adapted to local needs. Therefore, pathways between schooling and work must be worked out through collaboration between schools, the public sector, communities and municipalities, in order to help young people find jobs or return them to school or training institutions that better prepare them for the local labour market.

2.8 Rising Unemployment and the Youth Urban Divide

With the current economic downturn, youth-specific labour market issues might remain unaddressed since little progress has been made during the more prosperous years. ILO Global Employment Trends 2009 show that globally, the number of unemployed young people has increased to 76 million[28] – or almost 50 per cent of the total number of unemployed. Global trends suggest that little progress has been made to improve the position of young people in labour markets, and they still suffer disproportionately from a lack of decent work opportunities. Almost 300 million young people count among the "working poor" – they are unskilled, in insecure jobs and working in unsatisfactory conditions. In other words, even when employed, millions are not in decent jobs that offer dignity, opportunity and security. ILO projections on youth labour show that sub-Saharan Africa, South and South East Asia, and the Pacific will have the largest numbers of working poor young people by 2015 (see Table 2.2).

Jobs remain young people's fundamental challenge

Moving from school to a job, from parents' homes to marriage and own households, from a dependent status to one where one's voice matters in the community is what marks the transition from adolescence to adulthood. If a young person seeking work fails to find any and is unable to set themselves up in productive, decent livelihoods, s/he can become socially excluded and enter a cycle of poverty.

Young people's life chances, including the possibilities of securing good jobs or establishing viable businesses, are affected by the economic standing of their parents. Intergenerational inequalities can mean the persistence of inferior opportunities for particular groups of people. Inequalities in wealth and inequality of power are related.

TABLE 2.2 **GLOBAL AND REGIONAL ESTIMATES AND PROJECTIONS OF THE YOUTH LABOUR FORCE, 2005 AND 2015 (THOUSANDS)**

Region	Youth labour force in 2005	Youth labour force in 2015	Change (2005-2015)
Developed economies	64 501	61 167	-3 334
Central and Eastern Europe (non-EU) and CIS	29 661	23 989	-5 672
East Asia	154 511	139 596	-14 915
South-East Asia and the Pacific	61 490	72 889	11 399
South Asia	136 616	148 293	11 677
Latin America and the Caribbean	57 149	56 649	-500
Middle East and North Africa	33 174	34 039	865
Sub-Saharan Africa	96 153	120 587	24 434
World	633 255	657 209	23 955

Source: International labour force, Global Employment Trends for Youth 2006 (Geneva: International Labour Organization, August 2006).

Even at the individual level, a young person's sense of social status and personal "power" is connected to what they are able to earn and spend. If "productive" ways of earning such power and status are not easily available, even illegal and dangerous means of securing money become attractive.

The following sub-section outlines the status of youth employment in sub-Saharan Africa, South Asia and Latin America.

Sub-Saharan Africa

By 2015, the population aged 15-24 years in sub-Saharan Africa is expected to reach some 200 million, and the population aged 15-34 is projected to be 343 million.[29] Sub-Saharan Africa is the only region in the world that has registered a sharp increase in the total number of young working poor (those subsisting on less than US$ 1 per day). Between 1995 and 2005, the number of such individuals rose from 36 million to 45 million[30]. It is estimated, for example, that over 90 per cent of Nigerian youth live on less than US $2 per day. Many are food-insecure, lack access to clean water and electricity and live in sordid slum conditions. This trend persists in other parts of Africa.

Asia

Although Asia has shown the most progress in terms of employment creation, young people in the larger urban areas continue to suffer from a lack of decent work opportunities. More than 50 per cent of the world's youth are in Asia. By 2030, the number of youth living in Asian urban areas is expected to rise to 533 million. The region's total urban population is projected to increase from 1,553 to 2,663 million, with the proportion of urban residents rising from 40 to 55 per cent of the global population.[31] In South Asia and East Asia, youth are almost three times as likely to be unemployed as adults. In South-East Asia and the Pacific, youth are five times as likely as older workers to be unemployed.[32] It should be noted that employment and unemployment figures conceal problems of underemployment and poverty among working youth.

The dynamism of Asian economies notwithstanding, labour markets have not always been able adequately to absorb urban youth, making this group more vulnerable to poverty and social exclusion. The relatively high rate of joblessness among educated youth seems to derive at least partly from a misalignment between the contents of their education or training and the expectations of the workplace, a phenomenon common to most countries in Africa as well. Moreover, the more educated are more demanding as to the kind of work they want. In India for example, the largest category among unemployed females is comprised of educated young women who spurn clerical work yet whose education is not specialized enough to be professionally employed or self-employed. [33]

Latin America and the Caribbean

Latin American countries have made impressive progress in providing young people with educational opportunities, but these have not resulted in better access to employment. Although young people face severe difficulties in the labour market, those between the ages of 15 and 19 are most affected in terms of income and unemployment. If they abandon school at that age, as many do, it is very difficult for them to find a job. In Brazil for example, unemployment for the 15-19 year age group rose from 13 to 23 per cent between 1995 and 2003. For those between 15 and 24 years of age, joblessness rose from 10 to 16 per cent over the same period,[34] or higher than the overall unemployment rate.

Unlike most other regions, in Latin America girls are among the most advantaged in reading and even mathematics.[35] Nevertheless, this educational achievement has not improved the position of young women in the labour market. Problems with unemployment and underemployment remain severe for them, who fare worse than male peers in terms of unemployment and wages.

2.9 Informalization of Urban Employment reflects Exclusionary Economic Growth and Quality Jobs

There is widespread recognition that the formal sector in the developing world is not able to provide adequate employment opportunities to young people seeking work. The inability of economies to create adequate numbers of quality jobs is one of the root causes of economic informality. When young people in urban areas do find jobs, they are often in family-owned businesses, small and low-productivity firms, domestic employment or the informal economy – all of which offer low incomes and little or no labour protection. However, cities can offer ways of improving the skills and knowledge of youth employed in low-income jobs or those looking for jobs. Mumbai's night schools offer an example (see Box 2.1).

BOX 2.1: MUMBAI'S NIGHT SCHOOLS FOR WORKING YOUTH

Mumbai has a long-established tradition of "night schools'"for working youth, mostly those in the textile, trade and hotel industries. These schools also cater more and more to a larger cross-section of the migrant youth population.

Some of the city's distinguished professionals have come from these schools. Youth-led non-governmental organizations are bringing new energy to this tradition.

Source : Karmayog website http://www.karmayog.org/bmcschools/bmcschools_10471.htm

The ILO[36] estimates that approximately 85 per cent of all new employment opportunities in developing countries are created in the informal economy. The informal sector is no longer the "alternative" economy. Yet, issues of legality, social protection and predictability remain to be fully addressed if the informal sector is to be recognized and supported as a legitimate arena of self-employment, paid work and skills delivery. Policy prioritization of decent work for youth is very important, as noted by the ILO.[37] If young people experience a lack of decent work at an early age, they are often permanently jeopardized in terms of future employment prospects and behaviour patterns as workforce members. The ILO[38] also sees a proven link between youth unemployment and social and economic exclusion. Social and economic exclusion may, in fact, be a determinant as well as a result of unemployment. Some municipal officials and stakeholders, such as in Nigeria, are becoming more aware of these realities (see Box 2.2).

BOX 2.2 THE GOOD AND BAD "AREA BOYS AND GIRLS" OF LAGOS, NIGERIA

In Lagos, the disgruntled youth of the 1980s were pejoratively referred to as "Area Boys and Girls" due to their constant troublemaking. They became a source of serious concern to successive administrations. However, thanks to joint public-private, voluntary, corporate and charitable efforts these young people have become the "Good Boys and Girls of Lagos". Their training includes poultry management. The Direct Labour Agency and other government bodies such as the Lagos Waste Management Authority offer jobs as technicians, drivers, highway managers, etc. In addition, "Operation Weed for Flowers" has involved over 1,000 participants. Other youth undergo various training programmes including animal husbandry, panel beating, etc.

Source: UN-HABITAT Survey, Lagos City Report by Boladale Abiola (UN-HABITAT, 2009)

2.10 Summary

1. The association between the level of education and urban opportunity and inclusion is statistically significant at a 10 per cent level, a finding that corroborates the widely known fact that better educated people enjoy better access to opportunities than others

2. Parental background plays a significant role, seemingly shaping any opportunities available to children and characterizing groups at the bottom of both economic and educational ladders.

3. This suggests a strong relationship between girls' primary education and mother's education in urban areas. In other words, mother's education is a significant factor in youth educational status, as educated mothers tend to promote their children's education.

4. The survey shows that the uneducated are the main victims of urban exclusion. More of the respondents with higher levels of education perceived their cities as offering opportunities to integrate. These findings point to education, and especially females', as a critical factor for access to urban opportunities.

5. Disparities based on wealth, gender, location, ethnicity and other markers for disadvantage persist in terms of school attendance, literacy and educational attainment. There are also alarming numbers of "idle" youth, i.e., those neither in school nor at work, and who are vulnerable to exploitation and incitement. Non-formal education and skills delivery that can offer a second chance to school drop-outs or the unemployed should contribute to the positive channeling of young people's energies and abilities.

6. Inequality of opportunity fuels social and economic exclusion manifesting strongly in high youth unemployment. Early school drop-out contributes significantly to youth unemployment, particularly among slum dwellers.

Enterpreneurship training for youth in Nairobi,Kenya
© **UN-HABITAT**

END NOTES

[1] Wolff, 2001.
[2] World Bank, 2007.
[3] Power et al., 2009.
[4] Lave, 1996, 3(3), 149-164.
[5] Kahlenberg, 2004.
[6] Ibid.
[7] Sen, 2000.
[8] UN-HABITAT, 2010b.
[9] UNESCO, 2009.
[10] Lugano and Sayer, 2003.
[11] Jones and Chant, 2009.
[12] Ibid.
[13] Jimenz et al., 2007.

[14] Jones and Chant, 2009.
[15] UNESCO, 2009.
[16] ILO, 2009.
[17] Ibid.
[18] UNESCO, 2009.
[19] UNICEF, 2007.
[20] UNESCO, 2007.
[21] UN DESA, 2007.
[22] UN-HABITAT, 2010b.
[23] UNESCO, 2009.
[24] UN-HABITAT, 2006a.
[25] World Bank, 2008.
[26] ILO, 2008.

[27] Cunha et. al., n.d.
[28] ILO, 2009.
[29] ILO, 2008.
[30] UN DESA, 2007. Ch. 3
[31] ILO, 2006.
[32] UN DESA, 2005c.
[33] ILO, 2006.
[34] Rustogi, 2009.
[35] According to National Homes Survey (PNAD), Brazil.
[36] ILO, 2008.
[37] Ibid.
[38] Ibid.

03

Family Resources as Drivers of Opportunity Inequality

Woman from the Ferguson Road settlement, Sri Lanka
© **Ruth McLeod. UN-HABITAT**

3.0 Introduction

This chapter builds on the basic notion that inequality of outcomes is defined by a multidimensional set of instrumental capabilities (including shelter). It is clear from the previous chapters that the negative externalities arising from social, political and cultural deprivations contribute to unequal opportunity outcomes. In short, all other capability deprivations are as harmful as economic and income inequality. Importantly, all the opportunity deprivation sets interact in complex ways and largely revolve around economic capability in ways that see causality flowing in both directions. For instance, social inequality, as evidenced in educational and nutritional deprivation, is certain to impair the capacity of an individual to lead a fulfilling and productive life, and can lead to *economic* deprivation.

Based on the differentiation of capabilities among urban dwellers, this chapter provides empirical evidence of the extent to which young people living in slum or non-slum areas are deprived of a number of services, such as shelter, water, sanitation and other basic infrastructure. For each of these, the extent of deprivation reflects various degrees of poverty, asset deprivation and, ultimately, inequality across the social, economic, political and cultural spectrum. For example, if one considers the relationship between poverty and access to safe water, the "very poor" may be unable to access piped water and have to content themselves with natural water sources, like rivers and streams. On the other hand, the "surviving poor" category can include those with access to public tap and piped water, albeit with varying degrees of accessibility.[1]

Each category of unequal opportunity features clear differences across individuals, households and communities.

For instance, a family in the "surviving poor" group but with access to piped water at home will seem to be better off than a "very poor" rural household relying on a fresh water stream. However, the urban family may be deprived of proper toilet facilities (using pit latrines rather than flush toilets) and proper sanitation. Such deprivations can combine in a variety of ways, but the emphasis in this Report will be on the broad empirical findings illustrating these various situations.

This chapter considers family resource proxies such as shelter (in both slums and non-slums), space and its impact on other instrumental capabilities (e.g., education), and access to basic services (water, sanitation and electricity). In addition, this chapter analyses the health dimension of opportunity inequality.

More specifically, this chapter focuses on macroeconomic correlations, such as between access to improved sanitation and safe drinking water on the one hand, and GDP (based on 2005 data[2]) on the other hand. Figure 3.1 shows the slopes in the trend lines illustrating the proportions of the population having access to improved sanitation facilities and safe drinking water (for background explanation, see Box 1.3). These positive slopes suggest an association between infrastructure variables and GDP. To some extent, this is self-explanatory, since countries with higher GDP per capita are expected to allocate more resources to the social sector, providing larger segments of society access to better infrastructure.

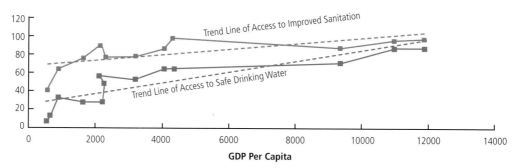

Source: World Bank, 2005

The association of GDP per capita with expenditure on health (per capita, same year) is depicted in Figure 3.2. The relationship is similar to that between infrastructure and GDP. This same argument explains the positive association between GDP and expenditure on health.

FIGURE 3.2: **GDP AND EXPENDITURE ON HEALTH**

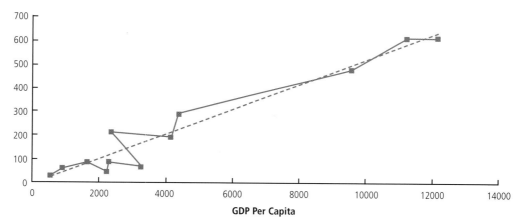

Source: World Bank, 2005

The relationship between GDP and maternal mortality (an outcome of health policies) is illustrated in Figure 3.3. The figure shows that mortality declines as GDP per capita increases. The results are, to some extent, related to the findings in Figure 3.2. Lower mortality rates can be achieved only through better health policies and more resource allocation to health care; these improved policies and higher allocations are, in turn, largely a function of overall GDP, i.e., economic resources. Figure 3.2 confirms that higher GDP leads to higher allocations to health services. This is what has enabled richer countries, for instance, to reduce maternal mortality.

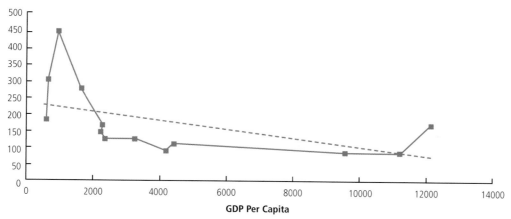

Source: World Bank, 2005

Figure 3.4 shows a negative association between female educational attainment and maternal mortality. Self-explanatory as this may seem, it comes as a very apt empirical demonstration to policymakers of the need to steer female education policies in a fresh direction. The statistical analysis in this sub-section suggests that improved educational opportunities for females could result in reduced inequality and more inclusive social and economic development.

FIGURE 3.4: **MATERNAL MORTALITY RATE AND FEMALE ENROLMENT IN SECONDARY EDUCATION**

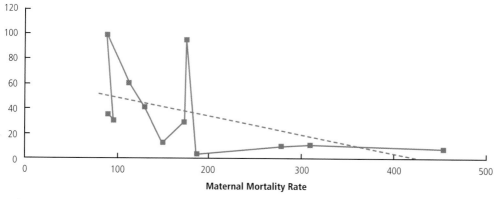

Source: World Bank, 2005

3.1 Shelter Inequality Determines Youth Access to Education

The shelter conditions of young women and men are closely related to differences in marital status, education and income levels. Largely regardless of specific cultures, youth as a transitional phase includes successive stages of living with one's parents, or alone, or with a partner, with or without children or setting up as a family. Access to living space is as much an expression of where a person stands in their transition to adulthood as of social inequality, since the problems youth face in the labour and housing markets are for a large part related to incomes.

Being typically first-time entrants into the housing and labour markets, young people are not among the most favoured in the credit markets either, except for a minority who are highly qualified and in formal employment. What emerged from the UN-HABITAT Urban Youth Survey 2009 is the distinct impact of the place where a youth lives on their life paths and employment (see Box 3.1).

It is well established that in some developing regions, urban dwellers – even those in slums – are supposed to have better access to services than people in rural areas.

Rio de Janeiro, Brazil combines overall prosperity and poor opportunities for youth.
© **Bigstockphoto**

Favela in Rio de Janeiro, Brazil
© **Gary Yim/Shutterstock**

However, due largely to economic, social and cultural segmentation, slum dwellers are denied opportunities to proper, quality education and by implication to fulfilling careers. Empirical evidence suggests that youth and children who grew up in slum communities are less likely to enrol in school and more likely to drop out, and many do not even attend secondary school. In many cities, the space divide is evident in the schooling profile of the large majority of youth, where there are differentials between slum and non-slum areas. Compared with the overall encouraging pattern of school enrolment, there is evidence that in many African slums primary school enrolment is decreasing.

In Eastern and Southern Africa, the most significant progress in school enrolment in the late 1990s was concentrated in rural areas, leaving out many poor urban families. In Tanzania, for example, net enrolment ratios increased in both rural and non-slum urban areas, but actually decreased in slum areas. The same worrisome phenomenon is evident in Zambia and Zimbabwe and is not confined to sub-Saharan Africa. In Guatemala in 1999, only 54 per cent of children living in slums were enrolled in primary education, versus 73 per cent in non-slum urban areas and 61 per cent in rural areas. The same situation prevailed in Brazil in the late 1990s.[3]

BOX 3.1: **DEFINED BY ADDRESS**

In Mumbai, India

"Every other divide is overwritten by the economic divide in Mumbai," said one participant. "The schools we go to, the skills we acquire, are all determined by where we live. And where we live is determined by our economic status. So, if I can only afford to live in a slum or a *chawl* [cheap lodging house], I go to a school that caters only to children from that locality." "We can never « belong », no matter what our caste or educational background." One's address says it all. "Even if I have money, it is not easy to break into elite circles if I happen to live in, say, a *basti* [shared habitation] or a *chawl*." Was this getting worse or better? Better, said most young local respondents. "Even slums like Dharavi [one of India's largest] are undergoing a transformation. And soon it will no longer matter where you live in Mumbai."

In Kingston, Jamaica

For many young people in Kingston's inner city, a main source of exclusion is the stigma attached to home addresses. Many of those areas are associated with gang warfare, crime and violence. As a result, law-abiding citizens, who are the majority, end up adversely stereotyped. Some youth acquire jobs based on false addresses on application forms, to try to avoid area stigma; but others have no such option, while others still refuse on principle to do that. Young people said that, even at graduate level, those students living in higher income areas will receive preferential treatment. On the other hand, females from the inner city tend to receive less of a negative response from employers when compared with their male counterparts.

Source: Mumbai and Kingston Youth Focus Group Discussions for UN-HABITAT Urban Youth Survey (UN-HABITAT, 2009)

The educational gap associated with economic status can be very substantial. In Bangladesh, Nepal and Pakistan, for instance, fewer than 40 per cent of children in the poorest socioeconomic quintile complete primary school, compared with 70 to 80 per cent in the richest quintile.[4] In Sierra Leone, the figures are 20 per cent and 70 per cent, respectively.

Among slum communities in Nigeria, children are 35 per cent less likely than children from non-slum areas to attend school. In Bolivia, only 10 per cent of children in the poorest quintile complete primary school, as compared with 40 per cent of children of non-slum areas, and 55 per cent of children in the richest quintile.[5] For urban young people, therefore, income opportunities and job prospects are clearly

determined by the places where they grow up and attend early schooling. Stratified educational systems confine the poor to low-quality schools because low-income families have no other choice. Clearly, such children's opportunities are limited from the start compared with comparatively richer families; this results in patterns of recurrent intergenerational educational choices for parents and offspring, a phenomenon also known as "decreased" or "stagnant" social mobility.

The distinct pattern of spatial health is illustrated by the wide differences in spatial density found in Nairobi, as shown in Table 3.1, although the pattern is widespread in cities of the developing world.

TABLE 3.1: **DENSITY INEQUALITIES IN NAIROBI**

AREA	Pop. density/ km2	Description	Change (2005-2015)
Kibera	49 228	Informal settlements	-3 334
City Centre	10 966	Main commercial area	-5 672
Parklands	2 490	Upper-/middle-income residential area with a predominantly Asian population	-14 915
Woodley	1 962	Middle-income residential zone	11 399
Muthaiga	481	High-income area that accommodates affluent classes	11 677

Source: Maps Geosystem, Maps (UAE), Sharjah, U.A.E

The structure of the Kenyan capital is a complex one (Table 3.1), making it difficult to sort out the distinct land uses of its surface area. The wide variations in population density reflect various land use patterns; however, the spatially divided internal structure is based in large part on land uses and income levels.[6]

3.2 Space Inequality exacerbates Gender Inequality

There are qualitative differences in female literacy rates between rural areas and urban slums in selected sub-Saharan African countries. As shown in Figure 3.5, differences in literacy rates between rural areas and slums are not very pronounced in South Africa.

However, in other countries like Ethiopia, these differences can be substantial, with rural literacy rates of 15.4 per cent,

compared with 64.7 per cent in urban slums in 2000.[7]

It is clear from Figure 3.6 that female literacy rates are consistently higher in non-slum relative to slum areas. In some cases, the differences are substantial. For example, in Guinea, literacy rates in non-slum areas are almost twice as high as those in slums (60.7 and 30.7 per cent, respectively in 1999).

A similar situation prevails in Benin, where only 32 per cent of those living in slums were literate in 2001, compared with 62.4 per cent of those living in non-slum areas. In other cases, the differences are less extreme. For example, in Rwanda, Zimbabwe and South Africa, the gaps in literacy rates among slum and non-slum females are smaller than 10 per cent.[8]

FIGURE 3.5: **FEMALE LITERACY RATES, RURAL AREAS AND URBAN SLUMS - SELECTED SUB-SAHARAN AFRICAN COUNTRIES**

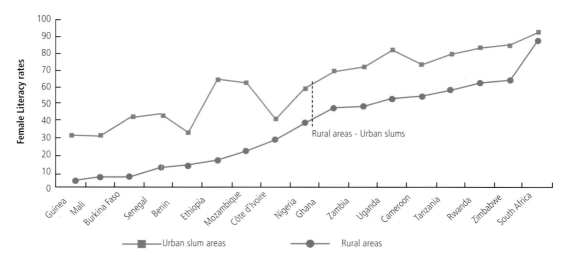

Source: Global Urban Observatory (UN-HABITAT, 2008a)

FIGURE 3.6: **FEMALE LITERACY RATES IN SLUM AND NON-SLUM URBAN AREAS - SELECTED SUB-SAHARAN AFRICAN COUNTRIES**

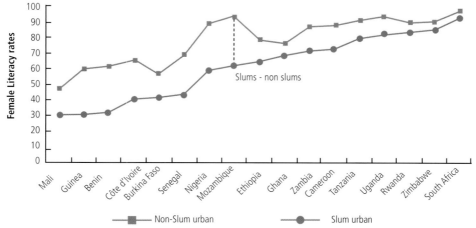

Source: Global Urban Observatory (UN-HABITAT, 2008a)

Spatial inequality has far-reaching consequences on outcome opportunities for young females. For instance, high rates of adolescent pregnancy and widespread female roles as domestic workers might be responsible for the differences in relation to women's participation in the job market. The distance to places of potential employment frequently combines with the stigma associated with location to confine young women to the place where they grew up, which perpetuates intergenerational inequality and stagnant social mobility.

3.3 The Health Divide as Inequality of Opportunity

Youth and, by extension, children born to families in highly deprived areas like slums have far less access to health services, such as immunization and, in some cases, antenatal and delivery care. For instance, in countries where a high proportion of poor youth and children are without immunization, national coverage can still be as high as 40 per cent, because immunization is much more widespread among the richest wealth quintile. In some countries, access to antenatal and delivery care is very unequal among slum and non-slum areas, but generally speaking the divide emerges most clearly in post-neonatal mortality rates. However, regardless of parents' economic status, urban children are still much better off overall than their rural counterparts.

The substantial differences between rural areas and slums with regard to health care are illustrated in Figure 3.7 by under-five mortality rates in rural and urban slum areas in selected Asian countries. Urban children tend to have a greater probability to survive the first five years of life than their rural counterparts. While in some countries, such as Yemen, Kazakhstan and Uzbekistan, these differences are negligible or non-existent, in other countries they are substantial. For example, in Viet Nam, under-five infant mortality in rural areas is 70 per cent higher than in urban slums.[9]

FIGURE 3.7: **UNDER-FIVE MORTALITY RATES IN RURAL AREAS AND URBAN SLUMS - SELECTED ASIAN COUNTRIES**

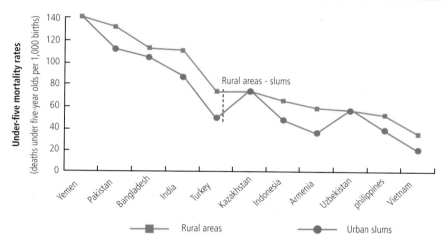

Source: UN-HABITAT, 2008b

The same kinds of disparities between slums and non-slum areas are observed in terms of access to health care services, as reflected in the differences in under-five mortality rates in slums and non-slums in selected Asian countries. As shown on Figure 3.8, in Turkey and Armenia the differences in slum and non-slum areas are negligible, while in India and Kazakhstan they are substantial.[10]

The poor access to health care among the urban underprivileged is illustrated by statistics from Delhi. Data from India's National Family Health Survey[11] shows that one in 10 poor children in Delhi dies before the age of one (94.4 infant deaths per 1,000 live births) and one in seven dies before reaching the age of five (135.5 deaths per 1,000 live births). Only one in four urban poor children are fully immunized and 70 per cent of urban poor mothers deliver their babies at home, resulting in high maternal and neonatal morbidity rates. Still, the total fertility rate among the urban poor is 4.8 – twice the average of 2.4 for Delhi as a whole.[12]

Not surprisingly, India's urban poor are more exposed to preventable illnesses. The incidence of communicable and vector-borne diseases is high among that category, with one in seven slum residents infected with tuberculosis. Incidence of dengue, malaria and chikungunya is also high.[13] India's public hospitals fail to provide adequate care to the urban poor. Waiting times are lengthy, which acts as a hidden economic cost and the quality of services is poor. These differences in access to health care, as well as the associated higher morbidity and mortality rates are not reflected in the traditional measures of income inequality. More specifically, Gini coefficients based on expenditure portray Delhi as a slightly more egalitarian city than India as a whole, with a Gini coefficient of 0.32 compared with 0.34 for India as a whole.[14]

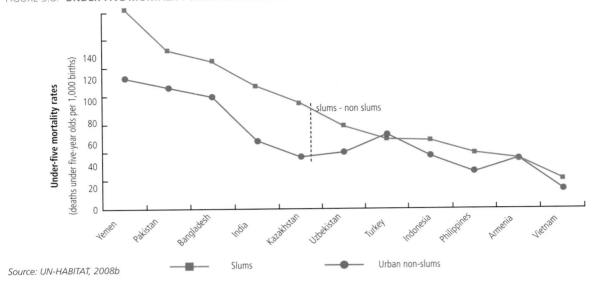

Source: UN-HABITAT, 2008b

3.4 Unequal Access to Basic Services as Opportunity Inequality

Poor sanitation, combined with unsafe water supply and poor hygiene, is responsible for relatively high mortality rates among slum dwellers. Poor sanitation is well known as the primary cause of water, air, soil and food contamination, and efforts to deal with it reduce the risk of diseases. Access to improved sanitation facilities can reduce diarrhoeal conditions by up to 37 per cent among un-served populations.

Based on the UN-HABITAT 2009 survey, Figure 3.9 depicts the association between the "Family Resource and Location" factor and basic services. Access to quality water and sanitation facilities during childhood is clearly associated with future opportunities and urban inclusiveness. The 53.86 per cent of youth with basic access during childhood do not consider themselves deprived of opportunities in their cities, while only 44.03 per cent of those who lacked such facilities in their childhood feel the same way. In other words, youth with greater access to better water and sanitation facilities during childhood tend to have greater outcome opportunity and are less exposed to pervasive inequality in their cities. The relationship is statistically significant (1 per cent level).

FIGURE 3.9: ACCESS TO QUALITY WATER & SANITATION IN CHILDHOOD AND COMBINED OPPORTUNITY INEQUALITY

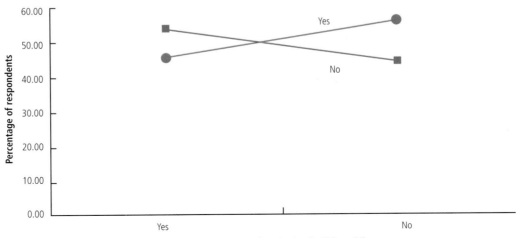

Note: Chi-square: 708.537; Level of Sig.: 0.000
Source: UN-HABITAT, 2009

The association between health and social services markedly transpires from focus group discussions, especially with the Nairobi group (see Box 3.2).

BOX 3.2: **LOCATION DETERMINES HEALTH AND BASIC SERVICES - VOICES FROM THE KAWANGWARE SLUM, NAIROBI**

Chris:

"I suffered from typhoid. For one month, we had no tap water. I was drinking water from the borehole. Even now, when you open the tap and water comes out, it is like a miracle. There is sewage everywhere."

Melchizedek:

"We have a water problem in Kawangware. Local authorities are trying to come up with solutions like treating water from the borehole. The normal water stinks. In this city there are two lines, one line that goes to the slums, for people like me, and the other goes to the other areas. My sister works in Lavington, and you can drink water straight from the tap there. In Kawangware, if you drink water from the tap, you will die."

Ian:

"Water has become like gold or oil. In some slums like Korogocho and Ngomongo, you find people who collude and block water from flowing to the people, so that people have to buy it at a much higher rate. They block the flow of water, literally. Initially, we were paying 20 shillings [or US $0.25] per litre, and when they saw it was making money, they raised the price to 30, then 50 shillings per litre. Then you wonder where they get the water they are selling, and as you will find out it is that very water that was blocked and diverted."

Samuel:

"In the town where my parents live, there is water shortage and rationing. They may stay for two weeks without getting water, because it is available when people are at work. The people there sometimes conspire with the water people to sabotage the system. They have no meters yet they get water. The system is wrong. It favours just a few people in society, the rich, the powerful and the well-known. One can be poor but well known and connected."

Source: Nairobi Youth Focus Group Discussions for UN-HABITAT Urban Youth Survey (UN-HABITAT, 2009)

A girl draws water from a dirty pond in Kyotera, Uganda.
© **SANA, UN-HABITAT**

3.5 Multiple Deprivations and Access to Basic Services in Slums

Access to services is not homogeneous within slum areas and varies broadly, based on the number of shelter deprivations. Those slum dwellers with the more shelter deprivations also tend to have less access to education than those less deprived, as illustrated by female literacy rates in selected sub-Saharan countries (Figure 3.10). For example, in Benin, the literacy rate among female slum dwellers with only one shelter deprivation was 43.5 per cent in 2001, compared with 23.9 per cent among those with two shelter deprivations and 6.4 per cent for those with three or more. This is equivalent to a six-fold difference between one and three shelter deprivations. Disparate literacy rates among female slum dwellers are also notable in Guinea, Burkina Faso and Nigeria, where the difference in literacy between those experiencing one or three shelter deprivations is roughly threefold.[15]

FIGURE 3.10: **FEMALE LITERACY RATES IN SLUM AREAS BY NUMBER OF SHELTER DEPRIVATIONS - SELECTED SUB-SAHARAN AFRICAN COUNTRIES**

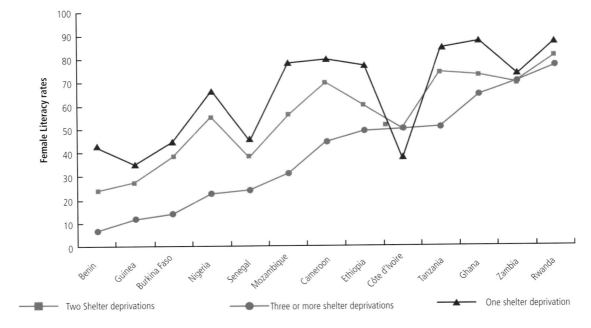

Source: UN-HABITAT, 2008a

Apart from literacy rates, the number of shelter deprivations can also be associated with differences in access to health care among slum dwellers. As illustrated by a group of selected Latin American and Caribbean countries, the health conditions of those living in more substandard types of shelter also tend to be more precarious, as reflected by the lower probability of their children surviving until the age of five. Figures 3.11 and 3.12 show that this trend is particularly pronounced in Brazil, where under-five mortality rates are over three times as high among children living in slums with three or more shelter deprivations than in those living with just one. These disparities are also very stark in Bolivia and Peru, where the multiple is 2.6. Even in Guatemala, where slum dwellers are relatively less at a disadvantage, the probability of a child surviving until the age of five increases by almost 50 per cent if s/he lives in a slum with one shelter deprivation by comparison with three or more.[16]

Differences in mortality rates are undoubtedly associated with access to health care (or lack thereof). Not surprisingly, the percentage of births attended by skilled health personnel is also correlated with the number of shelter deprivations. As shown on Figure 3.11, mothers living in slums with only one shelter deprivation are more likely to receive care at birth than those with two. Likewise, mothers living in slums with two shelter deprivations are more likely to receive such care than those with three. In all cases, the differences are substantial; where they are least pronounced, as in the Dominican Republic, they still amount to a 20 per cent difference between mothers with one shelter deprivation and those with three. In Bolivia, Nicaragua, Peru and Guatemala, mothers with only one shelter deprivation are roughly three times as likely to receive health care when giving birth as those with three shelter deprivations. This probability is almost five times in Haiti.[17]

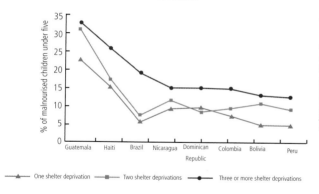

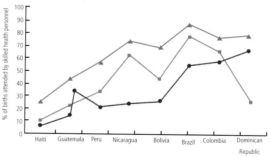

One shelter deprivation   Two shelter deprivations   Three or more shelter deprivations

Source: UN-HABITAT, 2008a

The number of shelter deprivations is often associated with more recently established slum areas. People in older-established slums tend to enjoy better access to services for various reasons. These include a longer lifespan over which some positive developments can occur, as well as better-established ties with the political system, and more central locations.[18] In India, for example, only those slums that have been officially recognized ("listed") are eligible for public services or slum improvement schemes. Likewise, older settlements tend to be more economically productive owing to their proximity to employment opportunities and markets, and lower transportation costs and times. As a result, residents of older slums tend to have a relatively higher socio-economic status than those in newer ones, as measured by education and income levels, occupational structure and housing conditions.[19]

3.6 Summary

This chapter demonstrates the multi-dimensional nature of opportunity inequality. An understanding of the relationships will therefore require a more nuanced notion of the different outcome opportunities. Although UN-HABITAT data indicate that housing conditions and access to basic services have improved from the 1990s onward, not only for cities as a whole but for those living in slum areas as well, great disparities persist between rich and poor. Those with the worst housing conditions also suffer from lower access to health and education. The specific findings in this chapter are as follows:

1. Youth and, by extension, children born within families living in highly deprived areas such as slums (and compared with non-slum dwellers within the richest wealth quintile) can have far less access to health services such as antenatal and delivery care as well as to immunization. Family resources expressed in terms of shelter (slums and non-slums) space have a significant impact on other instrumental capabilities such as education and access to basic services (water, sanitation, electricity). Infrastructure factors such as sanitation influence all the health dimensions that serve as measures of unequal opportunities.

2. Combined with unsafe water supply and poor hygiene, poor sanitation is responsible for relatively high mortality rates among young slum dwellers. Poor sanitation is the primary determinant of water, air and food contamination. Access to improved sanitation and safe drinking water is positively associated with national wealth as measured by GDP. Evidently, countries with higher GDP per capita allocate more resources to the social sector, allowing larger segments of society access to better infrastructure. In particular, this Report corroborates the association of per capita GDP and per capita expenditure on health.

3. Lack of family resources reflects in high maternal mortality, which is an outcome of city and national health policies. Mortality declines as a country becomes richer (GDP per capita increases) and allocates more resources to deprived areas. Youth in slums (i.e., shelter-deprived areas) tend to suffer unequal opportunity (high mortality rates) compared with cohorts from gated communities. The survey behind this report found that urban youth with greater access to better water and sanitation facilities during childhood tend to enjoy greater outcome opportunity and are less exposed to pervasive inequality further down the road.

4. Youth and children who grew up in slum communities are less likely to enroll in school or to complete primary or attend secondary school, and more likely not to complete schooling. The urban space divide is evident in the schooling profile of the large majority of youth in most cities who are enrolled in school: there is a large differential between slum and non-slum areas. Literacy rates for women are consistently higher among those living in non-slum areas relative to those living in slums.

5. Spatial inequality is an opportunity deprivation that has far-reaching consequences on opportunities of outcome for young females. For instance, high rates of adolescent pregnancy and the significant role of women as domestic workers might be responsible for the differences in relation to women's types of occupation in the labour market. This Report shows that the nexus of better shelter and

higher educational attainment for women results in lower maternal mortality. This provides policymakers with very strong empirical evidence in favour of reorienting policies related to female education in ways that remove disparities from a very young age and based on multidimensional factors. A combined statistical and qualitative analysis suggests that better educational opportunities for young women could result in more inclusive social and economic development, thereby reducing inequalities.

6. The shelter-related inequality of opportunity that defines the living conditions of young men and women are closely related to differences in marital status, education and income levels. Youth is a transitional phase where both males and females move from parents' homes to live by themselves, or with a partner with or without children and establishing a family. Lack of access to living spaces, a problem widespread among youth in the labour and housing markets, is for a large part related to incomes, which points to huge social inequality.

Unequal access to basic services: Indian girls and women collecting water
© UN-HABITAT

END NOTES

[1] UN-HABITAT, 2010b.

[2] World Bank, 2005.

[3] UN-HABITAT, 2008a.

[4] Ibid.

[5] Lockheed, 2008.

[6] Olima, 2001.

[7] UN-HABITAT, 2008b.

[8] Ibid.

[9] Ibid.

[10] Ibid.

[11] Agrawal, Srivastava, Choudhary & Kaushik, 2007.

[12] Chikungunya fever, which resembles dengue fever, is a viral disease spread by the bite of infected mosquitoes.

[13] Agrawal, Srivastava, Choudhary & Kaushik, 2007.

[14] UN-HABITAT, 2008b.

[15] Ibid.

[16] Ibid.

[17] Ibid.

[18] Although they were in the urban periphery when first established, older informal settlements frequently tend to be gradually engulfed into the urban fabric as cities expand over time.

[19] Ulack, 1978.

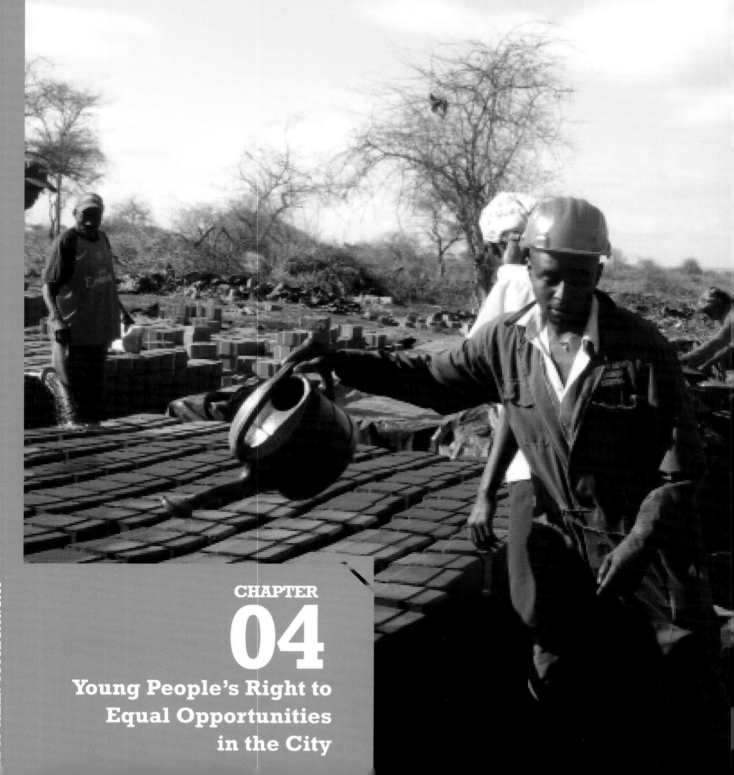

"Give us a second chance beyond formal education". Youth Empowerment Program Hydraform project, Kitui, Kenya.
© UN-HABITAT

CHAPTER

04

Young People's Right to Equal Opportunities in the City

> **"A right is not what someone gives you; it is what no one can take from you."**
> Ramsey Clark

4.0 Introduction

The notion of the "right to the city" has evolved in response largely to pressure from social groups and civil society organizations as a way of bridging the urban divide. This divide denies a large segment of urban dwellers access to the opportunities cities have to offer. The World Charter on the Right to the City supported by UNESCO and UN-HABITAT, among other agencies, comes as an attempt to relate urban deprivations to broader human right principles. Worldwide support for the notion has also led a number of municipalities to devise and endorse charters and other formal declarations to promote human rights in cities.

The "right to the city" subsumes a number of universally recognized fundamental rights that are endorsed, if only formally, in the constitutions of most countries in the world. Whether actionable or otherwise in any individual country, these rights are of a general, civil, political, social, economic and cultural nature. They are based on the principles of non-discrimination (including in terms of age, physical ability, racial or ethnic origin, etc.), "indivisibility of human rights, gender equality, progressive realization, non-retrogression, subsidiarity, solidarity, and cooperation".[1] Through these multiple dimensions, the right to the city also calls attention to issues relating to equality of opportunity for young people as well as for other groups with high propensities to social, political, cultural and economic vulnerability.

Rights are acquired in large part through the building of specific sets of individual and group capabilities. Chapter 2 stressed that development should look beyond individual human capital, production or higher output per capita, and also take in three mutually reinforcing aspects of human development, namely:

i. the direct beneficial effect of economic development on individual fulfilment and well-being (e.g., living free of sickness, earning superior wages, etc.);

ii. providing individuals the education they need to become effective agents of change; and

iii. building individual skills and knowledge for better contributions to overall economic production.

In other words, education is both a means and an end of development.[2] Therefore, youth is the greatest resource available to any society, and the most effective way of mobilizing this potential knowledge base is to deploy the right institutions and incentives for the sake of development.[2]

If this is to happen, the various dimensions of "rights" and opportunities must be viewed in a developmental perspective. When considering inequality, this Report looks beyond income and economic wealth in a bid to open up the black box of what constitutes poverty. This is why this Report examines the components of young people's "right to the city" and the way they interact, in order better to understand equality of opportunity as well as what youths value as desirable outcomes beyond income-earning. This chapter analyses five distinct rights, namely, (1) the right to equitable access to all basic services, (2) the right to avail of all economic opportunities and activities, (3) the right to voice political opinions freely, (4), the right to enter and enjoy all areas of the city, and (5) the right to all social and cultural facilities and venues. The effectiveness of these rights as perceived by young respondents in the five cities under review is measured on a three-point scale: "No right", "Average right", and "Full right".

Ranking Basic Services Deprivations

Figure 4.1 gives a graphic depiction of the most pervasive deprivations in poor countries, namely, the "right to equitable access to all basic services". The basic facilities include electricity, tenure, health, water and sanitation.

The figure shows that Kingston is the only one among the five cities under review where a high proportion (67.65 per cent) of young people enjoy equal opportunity of access to all the basic facilities (as measured by the perceived effectiveness, or otherwise, of their right to such services). Of course this ranking does not give any indication about the quality of service provision. For instance, while a city dweller may have

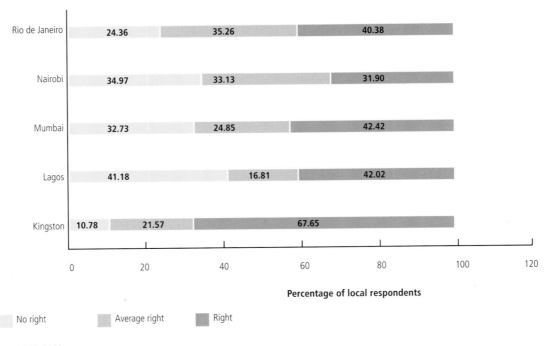

City	No right	Average right	Right
Rio de Janeiro	24.36	35.26	40.38
Nairobi	34.97	33.13	31.90
Mumbai	32.73	24.85	42.42
Lagos	41.18	16.81	42.02
Kingston	10.78	21.57	67.65

Percentage of local respondents

☐ No right ☐ Average right ☐ Right

Source: UN-HABITAT, 2009

"access" to electricity, the problem of power outages in a particular city location (e.g., slum vs. non-slum) may make fulsome enjoyment of electricity difficult. The same could be said of water supply, where "access" can as well be to high-quality supply through proper pipes or to unsafe well water of dubious origin. In contrast, in Nairobi, only 31.9 per cent, or half the proportion in Kingston, share this view.

In the three other cities, slightly over 40 per cent of young survey respondents reported equal opportunities of access to basic services. In Rio de Janeiro, the proportion of those who thought their effective right to such services was only "average" came at 35.26 per cent, the highest of the five cities under review. Over 60 per cent of all the respondents in the five cities believed that opportunity of access to basic services was equitable or only moderately so. For opportunity of access to basic services, Lagos was ranked the poorest. In the five cities under review, an average of about 30 per cent of young survey respondents said they had no equitable access to basic services.

The following sections review the perceived effectiveness of the various economic, social, political and cultural rights of youths in the five cities representing four major developing regions of the world.

Providência, the 'City of God', Rio de Janeiro, Brazil.
© **Mauricio Hora**

4.1 Right to Economic Opportunity

Six types of vulnerability[3] are widespread among the urban poor: economic, social, health, personal and psychological, as well as vulnerability related to housing and disasters. The urban poor are all the more exposed through an absence of mitigating institutions, including family and legal support.[4]

Figure 4.2 shows how local young respondents to the UN-HABITAT survey ranked the degree of effectiveness of their "right to avail of all economic opportunities and activities" in the five cities under review. Lagos (39.82 per cent), Kingston (39.58 per cent) and Nairobi (37.97 per cent) came on top.

FIGURE 4.2: **RIGHT TO ECONOMIC OPPORTUNITIES – PERCEIVED EFFECTIVENESS**

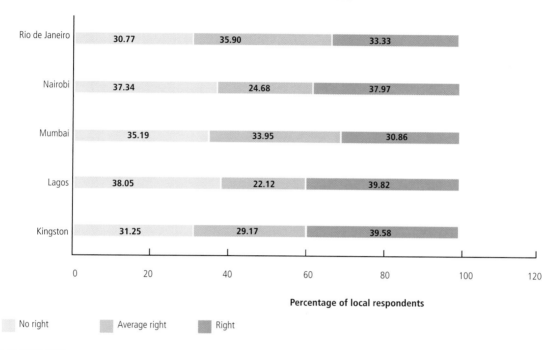

Source: UN-HABITAT, 2009

In Lagos, 38.05 per cent of young respondents to the survey found the city failed to provide access to economic opportunities, while a roughly similar proportion characterized Nigeria's economic capital as providing equal opportunities. This polarized pattern prevailed in Nairobi, too, with 37.34 per cent saying the right to economic opportunities was not effective, against 37.97 who said it was. Along with Mumbai and Lagos, the Kenyan capital was where economic opportunities were perceived to be most ineffective. On average, 34.60 per cent of all youths in the survey perceived that their right to economic opportunities was ineffective, but more than 60 per cent found it effective or "average."

Focus group discussions echoed the major findings of the survey (see Box 4.1). For example, in Mumbai only a quarter of the young respondents found the city "inclusive" in terms of economic opportunity. But half reckoned that economic prosperity was equitably distributed. When asked who benefited the most, one third mentioned the educated class, suggesting that education is a critical factor for access to opportunities.

Economic Opportunity and Inclusion across the five Cities

In **Kingston**, inner-city youth say a major source of exclusion is the stigma attached to their residence or place of abode (see Box 3.1). Inner-city youth make the link between unemployment and crime in two respects:

i.   unemployment increases vulnerability to illegal activities, and

ii. the crime and violence associated with gang warfare in an area causes businesses to close down.

This has happened in downtown Kingston, where many businesses have relocated to uptown areas. Crime, violence and the concomitant absence of peace are of greatest concern to half (48 per cent) of young respondents from inner cities, followed by unemployment (28 per cent). Youth from all classes agreed that lack of experience is an obstacle to employment even with a university degree.

Kingston and St. Andrew Corporation (KSAC) monument to child victims of violence, Jamaica
© **UN-HABITAT**

BOX 4.1: UN-HABITAT CITIES SURVEY AND FOCUS GROUP DISCUSSIONS – METHODOLOGY

In order to understand the conditions that define inequality of opportunity, UN-HABITAT combined a large questionnaire-based survey and focus group discussions with selected local young people. In the five cities under review, the focus group discussions brought together 20 to 35 young people aged 16 to 29.

In **Mumbai,** a survey was carried out with 160 young people who were selected through a purposive sampling framework. The group was 35% female. Around 76% of the whole discussion group had university education and most had well-educated mothers. A third of the fathers were in low-income, informal sector employment. The majority of the young people's focus group lived in middle-class neighbourhoods, and a small proportion in gated communities. While the sample may look small compared with Mumbai's population, it was still deemed apt to capture the nuances and diversity of India's economic capital in terms of inclusion, exclusion and equal opportunities.

In **Nairobi,** the young focus group participants were drawn from very poor low-income areas as well as middle-class and rich neighbourhoods, with the following population densities (measured as residents per square kilometre): Kawangware (45,139); Parklands (1,233); Kilimani (3,582); and Pumwani (10,175). The questionnaires were distributed across a much wider area representing all the five divisions in Nairobi: Central, Dagoretti, Embakasi, Kasarani, Kibera, Makadara, Pumwani and Westlands. Out of the 172 respondents to the survey questionnaire, only 20.35% ranked the city as 'inclusive' in all four aspects, while 79.65% found the Kenyan capital largely "non-inclusive," i.e., short on equal opportunities.

In **Lagos,** 125 young people responded to the questionnaires. They were drawn from various ethnic, educational, economic and social backgrounds, with a wide range of academic backgrounds (law, philosophy, international relations, economics, political science, computers, electrical engineering, etc.). Most were undergraduates or postgraduate students from two of the country's five best universities, and others from private and state universities spread across the major cities in western Nigeria.

There is also a consensus that contacts and "links" to people of influence are very important in obtaining a job. Upper-income youth specifically mention corruption and nepotism as challenges, even when an applicant is qualified for a position.

A considerable number of youth are excluded for lack of educational qualifications, and find that poverty-induced (at least partly) low school attendance acts as a hindrance. This may be due to the fact that families may not always have the financial resources required for new uniforms and shoes, or to provide lunch and pay for transportation. Where these deficiencies combine with other, multiple deprivations and lack of family support, the impact on youth can be devastating. However, upper-income young respondents concurred that school curricula should place greater emphasis on life-long skills to develop capabilities and build human capital.

In *Lagos*, the main factor behind economic exclusion is unemployment. In an effort to provide work experience, Lagos state authorities have launched a special jobs programme. The scheme enables thousands of young people, either still at school (during vacations) or just out of school (but unemployed) to indulge in various activities of a horticultural (planting flowers and trees) or public works nature (digging and grading of roads). This, according to the Lagos City Report, is to "keep them busy during the vacations; otherwise they are drawn to the street."[5]

Micro-finance also improves economic opportunities for young people in Nigeria's economic capital, as support to small businesses significantly reduces youth poverty. For instance, graduates of Skill Acquisition Centres can access small loans. In 2008, over 9,500 Lagos residents benefited from the scheme, but no age-disaggregated data is available.

In *Mumbai*, the main complaint among young people is that they lack information on employment opportunities. Few have a clear idea of the kinds of employment available in India's main economic centre, although opportunities range from the informal sector to labour-intensive to manufacturing (30 per cent of available jobs) to high-technology jobs. The poor information flow largely results from institutional failures and severely hinders young people's access to opportunities, with the repercussions this can have on other forms of exclusion.

Young survey respondents in Mumbai blamed this lack of access to economic opportunities on government and the municipal authorities in charge of various services and programmes. Although 67 per cent said government policies were creating new job opportunities, they complained that it was difficult to get relevant information about these or government schemes for youth entrepreneurship, or job-oriented training courses. When asked about economic opportunity in terms of accessible financial institutions, only 15 per cent of young respondents in India's financial capital perceived banks as "easily accessible," and another 35 per cent found them "moderately accessible".

Young respondents in Mumbai also blamed the lack of educational opportunities on lack of information. This was particularly the case with scholarships available from universities and other institutions. The situation is detrimental to most young people, but affects the poorer and more deprived groups to a greater extent as they have little alternatives.

What does the "right to the city" mean to young people in Mumbai? Most (88 per cent) understand it primarily as "the right to all basic services", with 50 per cent also including right of access to opportunities as well as to social and cultural spaces.

The *Nairobi* survey findings show that *the difficulty of securing decent jobs* is one of the major reasons for local young people's poor access to opportunities. Only 10 per cent of local respondents said they were employed, and the rest were unemployed with very few still at school. Such massive unemployment is officially ascribed to a combination of slow economic growth and rapid increases in the number of graduates joining the labour market. This situation is further compounded by the inability of both public and private sectors to accommodate an expanding young population.[6]

In the Kenyan capital, the focus group discussion provided very different viewpoints and experiences. Youth from poor areas harbour a deep sense of exclusion and inequality originating in family backgrounds characterized by lack of sustainable sources of income. Young people do appreciate that good education paves the way for better life opportunities and sustains their aspirations; but *parents' poverty and educational backgrounds prevent them from furthering their studies.*

Some of the young people agreed with the government's explanation for the current unemployment crisis in Kenya. However, others were categorical that the greatest hurdles to employment were prospective employers' requirements for "years of experience," along with nepotism and corruption. The comments (see Box 4.2) from two young respondents (one from an upper-class part of Nairobi and another from a poorer district) illustrate the impact of predetermined circumstances as well as parental education and social status.

Parents' education featured prominently in the reasons for deprivations and inequality in Nairobi. The mix in the participants from various economic backgrounds reflects in the different educational levels of their parents. In the discussion on access to education, a majority mentioned the importance of money in schooling. While the highly deprived believe that the system has not provided equal opportunity, those who are better provided see the educational system as also limiting in terms of lack of applicable knowledge and skills to equip them for self-reliance or self-employment, in the areas of business and entrepreneurial skills. The educational system has not prepared them for labour market opportunities. Youths with basic education believe they could have done more if trained to be self-sufficient instead of focusing on formal employment.

Another perspective, from **Rio de Janeiro**, features one of the lowest unemployment rates in Brazil, estimated at 7 per cent in 2006;[7] however, breakdowns of recent figures on work and employment for the 15-24 group are not available. In Brazil, youth unemployment is rising. For the 15 to 19 year age group, it rose from 13 to 23 per cent between 1995 and 2003, while for young people in the age bracket of 15-24 it rose from 10 to 16 per cent over the same period,[7] exceeding unemployment rates for the overall population and exacerbating the economic exclusion of youth. Available figures for metropolitan Rio suggest that the region is in line with the national trend, with youth unemployment figures higher than those for the population as a whole.[8]

Young people in Rio highlight the specific challenge they face between 17 and 23 years of age. They mention disproportional and fewer opportunities for economic advancement, in addition to the daunting task of getting through secondary education. A prevalent view is that youth are stigmatized in relation to race, gender, physical deficiencies and housing location, which become barriers not only when they are looking for work, but also with regard to access to education and quality of training.

Transportation is poor in Rio suburbs, and for this reason employers prefer youth who live nearer the work place in order to reduce commuting times and costs. Most young people end up with lower net incomes. Women are especially disadvantaged in the job market, as the government does not offer a viable system of crèches – and women are culturally expected to look after children and the house.

Young people, and the underprivileged especially, believe that there is a hierarchy of job opportunity that reflects a deep schism in a historically and culturally divided society. According to one focus group participant, "prejudices are very subtle and while a company may not offer a reason for denying one a job, it becomes clear when you look at who is offered a job and who is not".[9]

Informal employment...a young man hawks his goods in Liberia © **UN-HABITAT**

Employees on a construction site... formal employment for just a few?
© Stephen Coburn/Shutterstock

4.2 Right to Political Opportunity

The perceived effectiveness of the "right to voice political opinions freely" is assessed in Figure 4.3. Kingston and Nairobi score the highest rankings (45.83 per cent in Kingston and Nairobi 42.77 per cent) for perceived political inequality. This is contrary to what one expects to see in democratic countries, but shows how alienated the youth are, and how political participation is perceived in these cities.

Lagos, Mumbai and Rio de Janeiro are rated 38.74 per cent, 37.72 per cent and 26.45 per cent respectively on deprivation of political opportunity. An average of 37.65 per cent of all respondents believes political opportunity to be inequitable. However, in comparison, more than 60 per cent of the youth in the sample believe access to basic service opportunity is equitable or "average" equitable.

Political participation in **Kingston** tends to be blighted by the existence of "garrison" communities in poor downtown communities.

"A garrison, as the name suggests, is a political stronghold, a veritable fortress completely controlled by a party. Any significant social, political, economic or cultural development within the garrison can only take place with the tacit approval of the leadership (whether local or national) of the dominant party. The development of the garrison phenomenon is usually traced to the establishment of large government housing schemes in the 1960s and 1970s, where the allocation of units was done on a partisan basis" (Figueroa and Sives, 2003:65)[10]

From the early development of political parties and trade unions in the 1940s and 1950s, political rivalry has been expressed through physical violence. Gang warfare in inner-city communities has had devastating effects on community business, family life and community social capital. The main victims and perpetrators of this violence are underprivileged young men: male on male, poor on poor, youth on youth.[11] The situation is all the more complex as politicians wield less influence over gang leaders (they have fewer resources and are challenged by the drug trade). Nevertheless, many people still do not feel free to express divergent political views in these former garrison communities, many of which have armed gangs with dictatorial leaders or "dons" who run informal police and judiciary systems. Over half (53 per cent) of the youth surveyed from Kingston's inner city and working class areas felt the "right to voice political opinions freely" was completely or almost completely absent for them. Surprisingly, this also applied to 32 per cent of middle- and upper-income youth, suggesting an insidious and broad impact of political tribalism.

Political tribalism and its legacy of division (the "garrison" culture), along with gang warfare over turf (usually between community gangs, but sometimes involving gangs that are criminal and mercenary in intent) combine to blight economic opportunity and many other rights in inner-city communities. The violent, macho, individualistic *"donmanship"* culture which accompanies it is severely threatening in different ways to male and female youth. Inner-city youth felt strongly that police corruption was a major impediment to tackling crime because of the collusion of some police with criminals. Young people are not considered integral to the process of finding solutions and becoming part of the implementation of these solutions in Jamaican society.

FIGURE 4.3: **RIGHTS TO POLITICAL OPPORTUNITY - PERCEIVED EFFECTIVENESS**

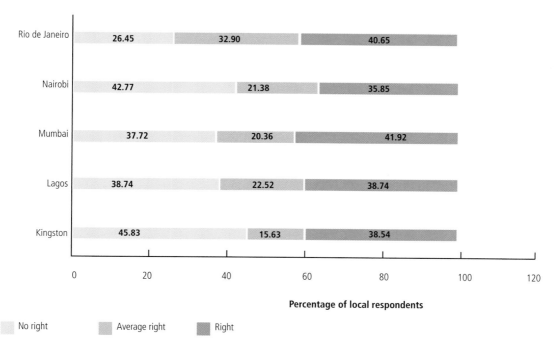

Percentage of local respondents

No right   Average right   Right

Source: UN-HABITAT, 2009

In *Lagos*, the imperative of democratization has opened up potential political space for youth. The government of Lagos state recognizes the *Lagos State Youth Forum* as the apex body for all non-religious, non-partisan, non-ethnic, affiliate voluntary youth organizations, clubs, associations and non-governmental organizations. At the district level, 57 local Youth Forums also represent the interests of over six million youth. However, the dominant political parties are yet to evolve mechanisms to mainstream youth participation.

In *Mumbai,* half of the young respondents reckoned that public administration is not transparent. Corruption is a main reason, according to a quarter of the respondents. A third mentioned bias in favour of particular groups, which they do not particularly associate with lack of funding or resources. The process of publication and public tendering was mentioned by 40 per cent of respondents, while a third said audits and reviews were a necessary step to transparent governance.

In response to the question whether policy implementation was participatory, half the respondents felt that it was indeed. Policy reviews, public discussion, monitoring and evaluation were the most mentioned channels through which such participation is fostered. Municipal reforms and policies are, unfortunately, seen by most as benefiting only politicians, bureaucrats and rich youth. However, a quarter of the respondents felt they really benefit no one at all.

About 75 per cent of *Kenya's* population is under 30 years of age but this is not reflected in political representation, as youth are marginalized and excluded from decisionmaking. Young people's understanding of political participation is directly related to the potential for tangible influence on matters that affect their lives and on public policy, instead of just being subject to these. Local young people also recognize that participation is an evolutionary process that takes time.

Young people in *Nairobi* identify two possible dimensions of participation: (1) collaboration with public authorities, although that depends on how much space government is prepared to open up; and (2) participation through monitoring and pressure by or from non-governmental organizations.

In *Rio de Janeiro*, young people rank the whole area as one of the worst states in Brazil in terms of political inclusion, for lack of local mechanisms for youth participation. Regarding potential channels for such participation, they mention councils and participatory budget procedures, but add that government does not encourage them. For young people, information is the key facilitator for participation. One respondent pointed out: *"people are not aware of a service and therefore are not able to influence it…"*[13] The Rio focus group suggested that the first steps towards participation would be (1) establishing institutions that provide information to grassroots communities, (2) decentralizing access to information, and (3) ensuring access to quality information.

4.3 Right to Social Opportunity

The "right to enter and enjoy all areas of the city" serves as a proxy for social equality as analysed in Figure 4.4. In comparison with the other cities, almost 50 per cent of youth in Kingston believe there is social equality in their city. The remaining cities are ranked as follows: Mumbai, 46.58 per cent; Nairobi, 39.62 per cent; Lagos, 37.50 per cent; and Rio de Janeiro, 37.50 per cent. The "average" ranking in this category is 41.87 per cent. For deprivation of social equalities, the highest proportion is 39.29 per cent, in Lagos, while Mumbai ranks last (27.39 per cent). The average proportion of respondents on the issue of social equalities in the five cities is 33.82 per cent. For social equality, the total proportion of youth that believe the social set-up provides "equal" or "average" opportunities is 67.17 per cent across the five cities.

Social inclusion is defined by equitable access to services. To young people in *Kingston,* this includes the following:

1. Feelings of insecurity in sections of their own community (inner-city and working class youth) or certain parts of the city (upper income youth);

2. Inaccessibility of community resources because of the territorial nature of community gangs in some inner city areas;

3. Insufficient recreational facilities, such as parks and places for young people to "hang out" and socialize; and

4. Vulnerable youth like street boys wiping windscreens; students with learning disabilities who are excluded by teachers; and functionally illiterate children who graduate from primary school.

Good social relations are extremely important in Jamaican grassroots culture, serving as a critical survival mechanism among the poor. For all groups except upper-income, their experience of supportive, sharing neighbours or friendly cooperative people, or good relations among peers, came first or second choices.

The first social inclusion issue raised by Kingston's inner-city youth is the lack of freedom to move freely in their own communities because of violence. Some fear going out at night, while others are unable to go to the other communities because of the territorial nature of the gangs. This sense of territoriality also affects community resources, such as football fields and training centres, which become inaccessible for everyone. In the inner city, considerable blame was put on police corruption for failing to deal effectively with gangs (as mentioned in section 4.2 in connection with political opportunity). For upper-income youth, security is a matter of concern if they are on foot outside their community.

FIGURE 4.4: **RIGHT TO SOCIAL OPPORTUNITIES – PERCEIVED EFFECTIVENESS**

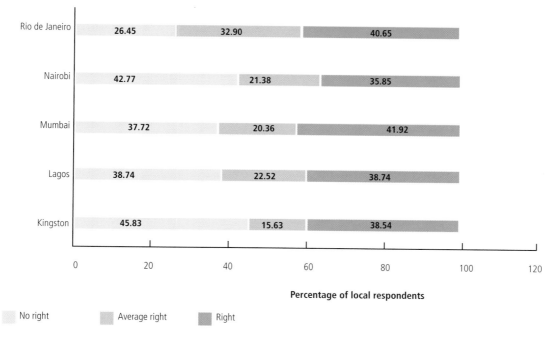

Percentage of local respondents

- No right
- Average right
- Right

Source: UN-HABITAT, 2009

Youth decorate their Youth Centre, Dar-es-Salaam, Tanzania. © **UN-HABITAT**

Regarding some aspects of education, inner city respondents were impatient with the pace of upgrading of high schools.[12] One focus group participant emphasized that this "is a major part of the urban divide; the population should be more mixed in school."[13] Upper-income participants were unanimously critical of the secondary school curriculum and teachers; they also criticized the university curriculum as too narrow and inflexible.

In *Lagos*, disgruntled youth in the 1980s were pejoratively referred to as "Area Boys and Girls" (see Box 2.2). Since then, adequate assistance has turned them into respectable citizens. For instance, since 1995, the Child Life-Line, a charitable, non-profit organization has been committed to the care and protection of needy children and youth, particularly in the Lagos metropolis. Apart from these actions from non-government bodies, state intervention has consistently offered training and employment programmes for youth. Given the scale of demand, much remains to be done. Young focus group members in Lagos said the local and state governments were sympathetic to the challenges they face.

Several initiatives and projects are supporting underprivileged youths and street boys. One example is the Skills Acquisition and Rehabilitation Centre, which has been expanded to accommodate more youths taken from the streets of Lagos. It was built to accommodate 1,000 but will now be host to 2,000. Hundreds of young beggars have been rescued and accommodated there. On top of this, 12 certified vocational training centres can train more than 500 students at any one time. Box 4.3 echoes comments from focus group participants in Lagos.

BOX 4.3: **SOCIAL EQUALITY AND INCLUSION: YOUNG VOICES FROM LAGOS**

"To say that these [training] facilities are in short supply in most of the cities in the country will no doubt be an understatement. Facilities are sparsely provided, only in some selected locations and accessible only to a few. A good illustration is the access fee to the only good and modern cinema in the city. The ticket, even though affordable to the middle income earner, is too high for those on low incomes. Recreation parks also share this same attribute". One participant noted that low-income groups were excluded from services: "...refuse collection facilities are only seen around the gated communities whereas slum dwellers have to walk a long distance to dump their refuse." Another observed: "...some areas live on borehole water supply provided through communal effort while power supply is unreliable." All the participants confirmed that public authorities failed to provide any social security or safety initiatives for young people.

Source: UN-HABITAT, 2009

In *Mumbai*, 70 to 75 per cent of focus group participants agreed that electricity, telephones and cable television services were mostly available. Only 40 per cent felt that services such as waste collection were well organised. Less than a third believed that recreational spaces, parks and gardens were moderately available. Public spaces such as seafronts, promenades, parks, gardens and open grounds are rapidly shrinking to be replaced by private clubs, associations, groups and services. This contributes to the exclusion of the poorer sections from recreational and sporting facilities and spaces. A young female teacher confirmed that "...this especially affects women, who cannot gather at street corners like men do."[14]

On the question whether social restrictions hindered access to public or private recreational spaces in Mumbai, a significant 42.5 per cent felt that social insecurity and vulnerability were a factor. Very few mentioned affordability or physical distance as an issue.

In Mumbai, social exclusion does not seem to be perceived as based on caste or religion. Focus group participants said it was rare to find friends' groups based on caste lines. On the other hand, they pointed out that the city has always had neighbourhoods with regional tags: Matunga (in central Mumbai) is South Indian or "Madrasi"; Santacruz (a western suburb) is Gujarati; and Bandra (another western suburb) is Christian.

Local young people are intensely aware of Mumbai's egalitarian ethos. "In my home town, I would not have been able to do all the things I am doing here. Mumbai is a city that offers huge opportunities for all", said a participant who had just started working after graduation.[15]

In *Kenya*, the *National Youth Policy*[16] has identified the eight strategic areas that must be addressed if young people are to be better integrated: (1) employment creation; (2) health; (3) education and training; (4) recreation, leisure and community service; (5) the environment; (6) crime and drug abuse; (7) the media and ICTs (information and communication technologies); and (8) youth empowerment and participation in national life.

Nevertheless, municipal authorities in *Nairobi* lack the capacity as well as the human and financial resources to expand social services. This is why a majority of urban youth tend to survive at the margins in a very precarious social environment. Inadequate and sometimes non-existent services, with their attendant health and hygiene hazards, have adverse effects on young people, who feel that the government is not interested in their welfare. Some of the youth in the Nairobi focus group also expressed concerns about the exclusivity of social infrastructures like shopping malls, public parks and cinemas. With reference to the public parks, many said they are not safe due to the risk of mugging unless you are in a group. The government has made an attempt to address this with policemen stationed in various parts of parks.

Young people from the poorer areas of Nairobi also feel excluded and many do not think the system wants them to be part of it, due to their lack of access to certain facilities. While some have never heard of the existence of some of the social facilities, others have but do not feel they can go there as they would not be able to afford anything. One gave the example of a guard outside a restaurant who discouraged them from entering, saying they could not afford anything in there. One youth said he excluded himself from the local shopping mall; he feels out of place when he sees the "posh" [i.e., luxury] cars parked everywhere, and perceives the place as one for the rich only. Another said that "...at the local mall, the guards have been trained just to visualize people. If you stand there for 2 minutes, they can ask you to move away. But white people come and can just stand there... there is a sense of racism here." [17]

The challenges for youth in Nairobi are similar to those in *Rio de Janeiro*. One difference is that in Rio, social inclusion is understood in terms of shelter, especially for the poorer segments of society who have little access to housing. It is most common for a young person to rent or build on the family terrain, as confirmed by a focus group participant in Rio, adding that "...the young woman stays at home. The young man builds on top of his father's house." [18] Some go into drug trafficking because they want to be independent. "...Loans are available, but creditors expect applicants to be in formal employment. Housing policies in general do not offer any specific plans for youth to own houses, and therefore it takes a very long time for them to be able to purchase one." The youth in the focus group agreed that while there are many programmes, none cater to the less privileged or the most deprived who hardly ever have a steady income.

Young people mentioned the *Favela Bairro*, [19] where the lack of maintenance led to structural problems related to water supply (despite this, they recognize that water networks do exist and there is good drainage). A common complaint about government housing was its lack of basic infrastructure or transport facilities. In addition, political disputes between politicians from different parties lead to lack of continuity in projects. Housing and urbanization programmes are treated as mere electoral issues.

An important historical issue in Rio has to do with the differences between poorer communities from the south zone and those in the rest of the city. Some are nearer the city centre, and therefore have better access to infrastructure and public services, and transportation is less of a problem.

4.4 Right to Cultural Opportunity

This final section focuses on the "right to all social and cultural facilities and venues", which is used to assess cultural equality (see Figure 4.5). As with "full access to basic services", Kingston is where the highest proportion (62.38 per cent) of respondents found that their right to cultural equality was effective.

Next came Mumbai (46.20 per cent), Nairobi (40.99 per cent) and Rio de Janeiro (37.01 per cent). The lowest proportion (31.03 per cent) was found in Lagos. On average, 42.75 per cent of young respondents in the five cities under review said their rights to cultural equality were effective.

In **Kingston**, the richness of the grassroots folk culture is widely acknowledged and appreciated across the social spectrum; it is officially celebrated every year through the Festival Competitions run by the official Jamaican Cultural Development Commission (JCDC).

Kingston features many venues for the performing and visual arts, making for a vibrant cultural life. Jamaica's renowned popular music tradition – originating in Kingston's inner cities – is fully expressed in concerts all over the island throughout the year. Backstage support for these concerts is a source of part-time employment, especially for young men from the inner city.

Sport in all its forms is extremely popular with Jamaicans. Inner cities provide the spaces required for football, basketball and netball. Schools raise money to send their teams to compete in the United States of America. This local support has contributed to Jamaica's international athletic prowess. Sports, especially athletics, are a source of upward mobility for poor youth generally, while football has played this role for talented inner-city male youth in particular. Sports are instrumental in building communities, as confirmed by a participant in the Kingston focus group: *"The one thing that brings the community together is the football team."*

Culture is the most inclusive of the four dimensions of inequality. Perhaps the most significant instrument of social exclusion in Kingston is language, and the different values accorded to standard English and Patois. Many Jamaicans are still ignorant of the fact that Patois, which is the first language of the majority of Jamaicans, features an African syntax. Still, it is viewed as dialect or pidgin and definitely considered inferior by many.

"Survival of the fittest "...equal opportunity must be combined with preparation and hardwork. Usain Bolt of Jamaica won the100 metres to set a new world record at the Beijing Olympics 2008.
©Pete Niesen/Shutterstock

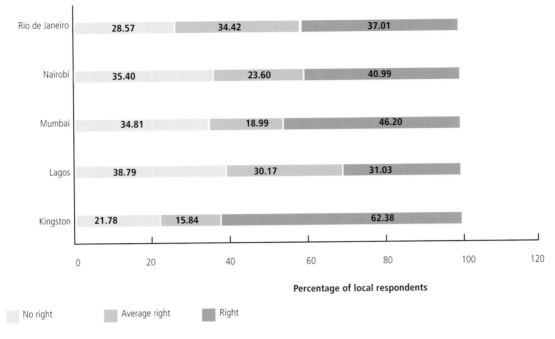

	No right	Average right	Right
Rio de Janeiro	28.57	34.42	37.01
Nairobi	35.40	23.60	40.99
Mumbai	34.81	18.99	46.20
Lagos	38.79	30.17	31.03
Kingston	21.78	15.84	62.38

Percentage of local respondents

■ No right　　■ Average right　　■ Right

Source: UN-HABITAT, 2009

Girls play netball at the Kampala Youth Centre, Uganda
© **UN-HABITAT**

In **Lagos**, a majority of young people reckon their city recognizes and promotes general cultural rights. People from different ethnic groups freely use their own language and hold cultural festivals all year round. A Lagos focus group participant referred to the "National Youth Service Corps" as a major national government initiative that promotes cultural diversity among young people. However, "elderly people, slum dwellers and the uneducated are no doubt marginalized from access to whatever opportunities are provided for cultural integration", he added.

Mumbai is a very inclusive city from a cultural point of view, according to local focus group participants. It is, after all, the film and entertainment capital of India. The film world allows entry to everyone and does not discriminate on the basis of region, class or community. Mumbai is a city with people from a variety of cultural backgrounds and everyone wants to know and enjoy other cultures as well.

Most young people in Mumbai reckoned the city promotes and recognizes their cultural rights. A majority concurred that ethnic groups were free to use their respective languages and cultural expressions and organize their own festivals. The city accommodates new forms of interaction. Celebration of specific cultures, shared cultural space and accommodation of cultural symbols in planning were all seen as proper municipal initiatives for the promotion of cultural equality and expression.

While the direct questions in the UN-HABITAT survey elicited predictable answers, multi-factoral analysis pinpointed some undercurrents that cannot be fully captured in such a small sample. It is clear that at both ends of the economic spectrum, for the poor and the very rich, **Mumbai** is not inclusive. While this reflects the middle-class nature of the city, it is also an indication that those on low incomes are poorly integrated, if at all, in the socioeconomic and cultural mainstream (see also Box 4.4)

Survey results from **Nairobi** suggest that culture plays a critical role in Kenya, too. Still, the Kenya Ministry of State for National Heritage and Culture appears to have been underfunded since it was established in 2007/08, with a budget allocation for provisional development expenditure amounting to Kshs 170.72 million (or US $2.27 million), which nearly doubled to Kshs 331.56 million (or US $4.41 million) in 2008/09. It will probably take some time before the fledgling ministry develops the capacities required to influence the policy process.

Participants in the Nairobi focus group stressed the importance of cultural heritage, but many felt that the capital's cultural development was restricted by a variety of factors such as lack of capital investment, leisure and recreational centres. Any facilities currently available are expensive for young people, including the National Theatre and the Bomas of Kenya. Some participants said they had to find a balance between meeting their basic needs and saving for cultural activities.

BOX 4.4: ECONOMIC, SOCIAL AND CULTURAL EXCLUSION OF VARIOUS GROUPS – PERCEPTIONS IN THE FIVE CITIES

The comparative ranking of the degrees of exclusion for various groups with respect to economic, social and cultural equality and expression give surprising and noteworthy results.

Regarding *slum dwellers*, more young respondents rated them as "fully excluded" than "least excluded" overall. But with respect to economic equality, more young people rated them as "fully included." On cultural exclusion, too, more young people rate slum dwellers as being most excluded than least excluded. To summarize, slum dwellers are more likely to be disadvantaged due to cultural than economic exclusion.

By the same reading, *youth of specific racial backgrounds* are more likely to be disadvantaged with respect to social exclusion than economic.

Disabled youth are more likely to be economically than socially or culturally excluded.

Elderly people are less likely to be disadvantaged economically than socially or culturally.

Uneducated young people are more likely to be disadvantaged economically than socially or culturally.

Young people from low-income backgrounds are more likely to be more excluded socially than economically or culturally.

Foreign immigrants are more likely to be excluded culturally than socially.

Migrants from rural backgrounds are more likely to be fully included socially than culturally.

These characteristics combined suggest that there is a distinct social and cultural divide that may not be fully acknowledged or accounted for. This calls for further inquiries and adequate measures to bridge these gaps.

Source: Focus Group Discussions from UN-HABITAT Survey

(UN-HABITAT, 2009)

The focus group also emphasized the need to teach cultural issues, especially with regard to appreciation of other cultures, in order to enhance national cohesion. This would also help to contain tribalism. This phenomenon, according to some participants, is so deeply ingrained in Kenyan society that it will take a long time to reduce, especially in cities like Nairobi. Tribes stand as incarnations of the culture and norms of a particular set of people. However, focus group participants felt that the national cohesion required for a "Kenyan" culture may be detrimental to tribal cultural identities.

Rio de Janeiro is also reputed around the world for its intense cultural life in all its various forms and spatial features. Cultural inclusion is favoured by convergent policies on the part of federal, state and municipal authorities.

A federal statute for the promotion of culture (Law N° 8313 of 23rd December 1991) established Brazil's National Programme for the support of Culture (PRONAC).

The law provides the legal foundation for the promotion, protection and recognition of national cultural expressions. The highlight of the law is a set of tax incentives that make it possible for businesses and individuals to claim refunds when they are involved in cultural activities. A number of local cultural initiatives aimed at young people benefit from the policy, although there is no information to determine how effective it is.

4.5 Summary

The findings in this chapter are as follows:

1. Fairly large proportions of young survey respondents reckoned that their respective cities were economically, politically, socially and culturally deprived.

2. An average 30 per cent rank the five cities as failing to provide equal access to basic facilities.

3. 35 per cent of young survey respondents had a similar opinion regarding equality of economic opportunities.

4. The following proportions of respondents believed that their cities provided unequal access to: political opportunities, 37.65 per cent; social opportunities, 33.82 per cent; and cultural opportunities, 32.32 per cent.

5. The Young people highlighted a number of anomalies in youth-related policies and implementation that exacerbate the challenges they already face. Their distrust of those in charge of urban governance is highlighted in extracts from the focus group discussions held in the five cities.

The major conclusions from survey returns and focus group discussions are as follows:

1. *National policies are not endorsed by lower administrative tiers*: Youth policies are national but in the five cities under review, youth-related projects are administered through provincial/state or municipal resources. National policies are usually not endorsed by the government echelon in charge of resource allocation to youth programmes.

This obviously creates a serious gap in terms of commitment to results. The local level is where young people either do or do not experience equality of opportunity. Only well-adapted, locally relevant policy frameworks can provide the incentives required for innovative youth-related programmes on the ground.

2. *Coordination across policies and sectors*: National and provincial/state governments in all the sample countries make programmes and resources available for youth development. But these efforts must be complemented by cross-sector and cross-ministry coordination. This is usually missing.

3. *Support to youth has a narrow focus*: As shown in preceding chapters, the determinants of inequality are multi-dimensional, including access to basic services and good quality of education. Yet government responses are often targeted at only two or three main areas of youth activity: skills acquisition, sports and, at times, access to micro-credit and project-related jobs. The extent of demand and shortcomings is usually too high for small steps to have any significant impact on the conditions of young urban residents.

4. *Policies are not targeted*: Youth policies often come in generic formats devoid of specific approaches to different types of disadvantage. In most of the policies sampled in the Appendix, there does not appear to be any focus on young peoples' rights or the best ways of strengthening youth awareness of and advocacy for these.

5. *Lack of trust in municipal and law-enforcement officials*: Young respondents in the five cities felt that public policies were not doing enough for them. Politicians were not perceived as people of integrity, but the occasional sympathizer or champion was acknowledged. Overall, police were not seen as sympathetic to or supportive of young people.

Due to lack of a proper ground, youth play soccer on the road in Brazil.
© **Lazer no Conjunto Prestes Maia UN-HABITAT**

END NOTES

1 Rights-based approaches to an inclusive city, including the right to the city, are discussed in further detail in UN-HABITAT (2010a), Ch. 3.1.

2 Sen, 1999.

3 As defined by the Asian Development Bank, these six types of vulnerability include: (1) economic vulnerability (low paid work, lack of access to credit on reasonable terms, legal constraints to self-employment); (2) social vulnerability (low education, lack of skills, exclusion from local institutions); (3) health-related vulnerability; (4) vulnerability to disasters; (5) housing-related vulnerability (lack of tenure, unhealthy and unsanitary living conditions); and (6) personal and psychological vulnerability (proneness to violence and intimidation to women, lack of information, etc.).

4 World Watch, 2007:154.

5 UN-HABITAT, 2009.

6 The Kenya Government Economic Survey 2009 (KNBS, 2009) shows a decline in employment creation from 485.5 thousand in 2007 to 467.3 thousand in 2008, and this situation is expected to worsen.

7 Instituto Pereira Passos, 2008.

8 According to the National Homes Survey (PNAD).

9 ISER Assessoria, 2006.

10 Figueroa & Sives, 2003:65.

11 UN-HABITAT, 2009.

12 Planning Institute of Jamaica with the Ministry of Foreign Affairs (2009), p. 4.

13 UN-HABITAT, 2009.

14 In Jamaica, there are wide differences in resource allocations and institutional academic expertise among high schools. Entry into high school is based on examinations at the end of primary school. Still, the best-performing primary schools are well-resourced private institutions which charge high fees.

15 UN-HABITAT, 2009.

16 Ibid.

17 Government of Kenya, Ministry of Youth Affairs and Sports, 2007.

18 UN-HABITAT, 2009.

19 Ibid.

20 Favela Bairro is a slum upgrading programme launched in 1993 and since then deployed in more than 150 favelas and other informal settlements.

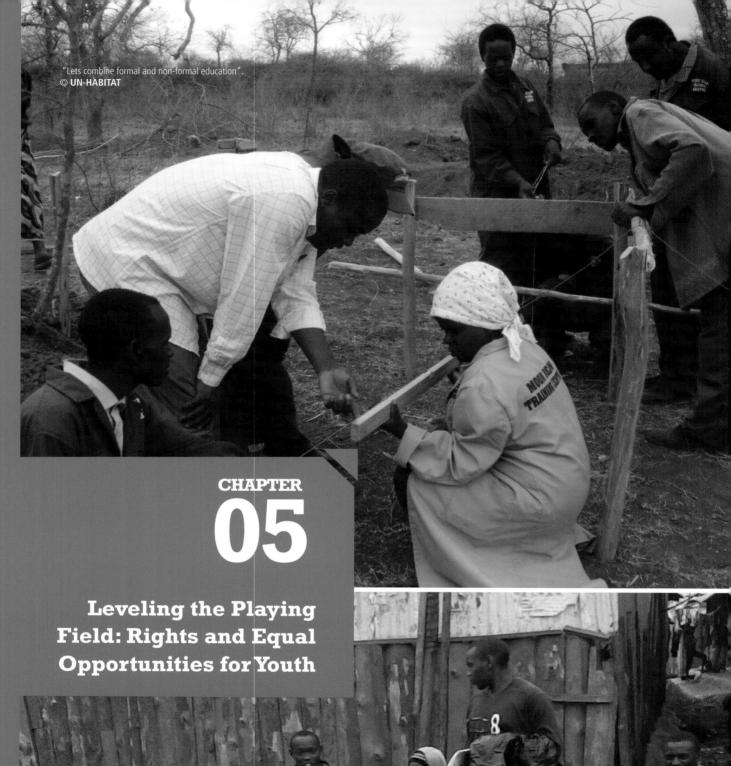

"Lets combine formal and non-formal education".
© UN-HABITAT

CHAPTER
05

Leveling the Playing Field: Rights and Equal Opportunities for Youth

Garbage collection remains a challenge in many African cities.
Youth group members clean up their neighbourhood, Nairobi, Kenya
© UN-HABITAT

> **I shall assume, then, that the purpose of an equal-opportunity policy is to level the playing field. What features, in the backgrounds of individuals in question, correspond to the moulds and troughs in the playing field that should be levelled off? I propose that these are the differential circumstances of individuals for which we believe they should not be held accountable.**
> John E. Roemer

5.0 Introduction

This final chapter summarizes the major findings deriving from survey results and focus groups, and proposes a set of policy recommendations to deal with the challenges facing youth in urban areas in the developing world. The survey undertaken by UN-HABITAT in five cities in Latin America, South Asia, the Caribbean and Africa shows that equality of opportunity and upward social mobility are affected by predetermined circumstances as well as intergenerational factors of social origin, as measured by parents' education and income status.

Supportive institutions and policies to facilitate equal opportunity are required if young people from the whole social spectrum are to have equal choices when facing the diverse opportunities available in the economic, social, cultural and political spheres. This, in turn, calls for enactment of appropriate national and international mandates and mobilization of resources at national and municipal levels. Youth-specific (i.e., dedicated) and youth-responsive (i.e., well-adapted to their conditions) policies, programmes, schemes and even business endeavours must be deployed. Various cities and countries can offer examples of such initiatives and interventions, but they are typically not broad enough, or far-reaching enough, to encompass the wide variety of deprivations that can be found at all levels of society.

The following are the major findings of this Report, followed by a review of key international mandates and the shortcomings of existing policies. In light of these and the findings of the UN-HABITAT Urban Youth Survey 2009, this Report proposes a number of policy principles designed to level the playing field for urban young people.

5.1 From Findings to Policies: How to Level the Playing Field

1. Policy must recognize the specific nature of youth as a period of identity formation and transition to responsible citizenship

If young people are effectively to move to responsible citizenship in their adult lives, they must be safe, healthy and engaged in a positive way in their transition years. Urban policies and interventions must recognize youth as this particular period of transition from school to the workplace, from parental to independent dwellings. Policymakers must be well aware that if young people are not adequately included in decisions on urban land, housing and employment, they are likely to express their frustration. Successful transition to responsible adulthood depends on leveling the playing field for social, political and economic opportunities, so that young people can build and maintain a meaningful sense of identity into adulthood. Cities should be able to offer this to their younger residents.

2. Youth-responsive policies and institutions call for capacity-building among urban decisionmakers and those working with young people

Local leaders, councillors, mayors and municipal officials have a critical role to play in the development of youth-sensitive urban mandates. They require training if they are to be able to expand broad-based youth participation in strategic urban planning and budgetary processes and to facilitate partnerships with key stakeholders. They must also be able to engage, analyse and respond in context- and group-specific ways.

Young people's capacity development should be linked to results that they and the relevant city specifically desire. Progress towards targeted results should be monitored. For example, technical and life skills training of young people should result in better access to opportunities for incomes, housing, services and land.

3. Education is a key determinant of opportunity equality. Therefore, more urgent attention and allocation of resources must focus on education, especially for girls and young women.

The UN-HABITAT Youth Survey 2009 shows that mother's education is a significant factor in youth educational status. Young survey respondents saw the uneducated as those most excluded in their cities. More well-educated than less-educated respondents perceived their cities as offering opportunities for integration. These findings point to education as a major factor if all young people, and females in particular, are to have access to the opportunities cities make available, and to take advantage of them.

Gender disparities in educational attainment are particularly obvious at the secondary and tertiary levels, where females are not at par with males. Disparities are also notable in school drop-out rates, with young women predominating, possibly due to adolescent pregnancies as well as socio-cultural pressures against girls' continuing education at higher level.

4. Review the Millennium Development Goals related to youth education targets

Governments should review the Millennium Development Goals as they relate to youth, and mobilize resources accordingly. Unless youth-specific data analysis becomes routine, and adequate local and national monitoring frameworks are established, there will be no tangible evidence on which to base or pursue well-targeted policies in favour of equal urban opportunities.

5. It is important to match education and skills training with the technical and vocational skills in demand on the labour market; and to offer non-formal options for the acquisition of education and skills.

So far, improved literacy rates and enhanced educational attainment have failed to provide more young people with jobs. Millions are either jobless or in unproductive jobs. Such provision of decent work to young people with employable skills remains a challenge for both the public and the private sectors.

Current statistics point to alarming numbers of "idle" youth (those neither in school nor at work) in Latin America, Africa and Asia. Non-formal education and skills delivery can offer a second chance to those who have dropped out of school or are unemployed.

6. Young people are deprived of multiple opportunities, and policy response must be multidimensional, too.

National sector-specific policies do not address youth opportunity issues, even though young people often comprise the largest section of urban constituencies. The UN-HABITAT Urban Youth Survey 2009 and youth-related literature show that opportunity deprivation sets interact in complex and apparently interconnected ways. For instance, the social inequality at work in educational and nutritional deprivation is certain to impair the capacity of an individual to lead a fulfilling and productive life, which can end up in economic deprivation. More and improved cross-sector coordination is necessary if youth-responsive policies are to achieve any impact. These policies must be part of broader efforts – of a social, economic, political and cultural nature – to bridge the urban divide and pave the way for inclusive cities.

7. Social and youth-oriented policies must also take parents' aspirations into account.

This Report focuses on objective causal links between parents' backgrounds and conditions on the one hand, and the opportunities these may or may not open up for offspring. Policymakers should be well aware of those links. At the same time, they should not overlook parents' aspirations and their understanding of the decisive role of education when it comes to securing better futures for their own next generation. Such aspirations from uneducated parents should receive adequate support from policymakers and local authorities if intergenerational inertia is to be broken.

8. Specific urban youth data is needed for sharper policy focus on the diversity of youth disadvantage and to promote equal opportunities.

The UN-HABITAT Urban Youth Survey 2009 showed sparse evidence of country- or city-specific data sets on youth or the degree of their political, social, economic or cultural inclusion. Most national surveys of well-being are carried out at household level, but there is a lack of youth-specific analysis.

9. Access to land and safe urban space is important for the protection, voice and empowerment of youth

The five cities reviewed in the UN-HABITAT Youth Survey 2009 featured significant degrees of youth exposure to risk and vulnerability. In some of those cities, social insecurity and vulnerability were found to restrict access to public areas. In any city, young people need places where they are sheltered, protected and mentored into democratic and economic processes. Peer exchange between privileged and disadvantaged youth from different urban areas can help create a united urban youth lobby and support system. In safe places – such as the "One-Stop" and "We are the Future" centres supported by UN-HABITAT – urban youth can access information and communication technologies (ICTs) as well as mobilize in favour of more effective rights.

Places where youth can access information are vital to their roles in urban communities, enabling them to engage in peer interaction, but such places require land. Serviced worksites where young people can upgrade their often low-productivity occupations and secure reasonable incomes require security of tenure. Youth-responsive housing and hostels need land, too. Once land use planning affirms the right of young people to a share of public land, governments can bring in partnerships for the establishment of information, training, health, production and recreation centres (a multipurpose centre can encompass all these) as well as for appropriate housing.

10. Need for better health policies

Reducing inequality of opportunity will require better health policies and more resource allocation to healthcare; at the same time, inequality of health opportunities is largely determined by shelter conditions, and therefore can also be tackled though proportionally higher resources for reduction of shelter deprivation in slums.

11. Specific policies for Shelter deprivation

Policymakers must deploy differentiated policies that target the multidimensional nature of shelter deprivation and its interconnections with a variety of health and educational opportunity inequalities. For instance, a special Educational Fund should be set up for youth growing in slums, with special attention to girls' education.

5.2 By Way of Conclusion

In this early 21st century, the world's cities are found to combine three interrelated paradoxes – some would say scandals. Never have such concentrations of riches, abilities and opportunities been so favourable to human development. Yet, all-too frequently cities also concentrate high, unacceptable degrees of inequality as these opportunities elude major segments of the population. This is the urban divide at its starkest.

The other paradox is that the opportunities that come with the "urban advantage" are more particularly denied to those, including children and young people, who have such obvious, vital roles to play in our collective future. This is all the more paradoxical as today, one half of humankind is under 25 years of age.

If there ever was a time for substantial, broad-based transmission from one generation to another, this must be it. Accordingly, this Report focused on the main obstacles which too many young people across the world are running against when looking to fulfill their potential and aspirations.

This Report comes with an implicit warning: poor circumstances for today's young people – the parents of the second next generation – will only perpetuate inadequate, or outright unacceptable, individual and collective conditions into an indeterminate future.

There can be no promising individual future at the margins of society, on the wrong side of the urban divide. Those well-educated but without decent jobs, if any, may vent their frustrations in criminal behaviour or outbursts of violence, while those with little education will remain hostages to grinding poverty and debilitating illness. Food to survive the day, but no health care to survive tomorrow, and no school to pave the way for the future: this remains the predicament of too many poor, underprivileged families in the slums of the developing world. How long do we want this to endure?

There can be no promising collective future in the absence of any positive legacy from and for everyone. This legacy takes the form of opportunities of all sorts, which give youth a sense of belonging with regard to the future. Education features prominently, as reflected in this Report. We pass the built-up collective knowledge of previous generations on to younger people who, by dint of talent, effort and inspiration, will enrich this legacy, in the process paving the way for a better, more sustainable future for themselves and for all. Enrolling the younger generations in primary, secondary and further education is tantamount to appointing them as our dutiful legatees.

This quasi-testament must include everyone in the younger generations, without any discrimination. This is not just for the sake of inclusiveness. Abilities and talent of all kinds are waiting out there, unrecognized, for the moment when they can emerge, take shape and benefit the rest of society – if only they had the opportunity. This comes as a reminder of the four main dimensions of inclusiveness. If young people are to shape our collective future, they require four main forms of opportunity: economic, social, political and cultural. Youth need these as they coincide with the four main dimensions of collective life, those through which they will manage our legacy to the best of their abilities and prepare it for the next generation – their own children.

Some will consider equality of opportunity and "leveling the playing field" as a way of introducing a degree of morality in the current, divisive dispensation that can be so tangible in modern urban areas. Others will emphasize the need to mobilize every available talent in the competitive "knowledge economies" which cities nowadays have come to epitomize. But then as we already know, the social consequences of mounting frustration in large, dynamic segments of any urban community can be detrimental to economic performance and success.

Far from imposing any new social order or hierarchy, equality of opportunity only aims at identifying and fostering individual potential, which inclusiveness in its four dimensions both channels and supports. Combined with an equitable give-and-take between current and successive generations, this process is also known as civilization.

BIBLIOGRAPHY

A

Agarwal, S., Srivastava, A., Choudhary, B., & Kaushik, S. (2007). State of urban health in Delhi. (Urban Health Resource Centre Report to Ministry of Health and Family Welfare, Government of India.) Delhi: Government of India.

B

Birdsall, N. (2006). The world is not flat: Inequality and injustice in our global economy. (WIDER Annual Lecture 9). Helsinki: UNU-WIDER.

Brown, N. A. & Jaspev. (2008). Forging a partnership between a private service agency and an impoverished but empowered inner city community. In Jamaica 2015: National progress report 2004-2006 on Jamaica's social policy goals. Kingston: Office of the Cabinet.

C

Charter for Women. (1997). City and shelter: Charter for women in the city. Retrieved from: http://www.cityshelter.org/03.charte/charter_en/charter.htm

Cunha, B., Santos, A., Damasceno, C.C.M. (n.d.). The occupational situation of young people in low income communities in Rio de Janeiro. Rio de Janeiro: ENCE. Retrieved from: http://www.iets.org.br

D

De Barros, R.P., Ferreira, F.H.G., Vega, J.R.M., & Chanduvi, J.S. (2009). Measuring inequality of opportunities in Latin America and the Caribbean. Washington, D.C.: World Bank.

Dowdney, L. (2002). Children of the drug trade: A case study of children in organized armed violence in Rio de Janeiro. Rio de Janeiro: 7Letras, ISER & Viva Rio.

E

Erulkar, A.S. & Matheka, J.K. (2007). Adolescence in the Kibera slums of Nairobi, Kenya. New York: Population Council.

European Charter. (2000) European cities conference on human rights. European Chater for the Safeguarding of Human Rights in the City. Retrieved from: http://www.ville-ge.ch/fr/media/pdf/Charte_english.pdf

F

Federal Office of Statistics. (2006). Population census of Nigeria, 1952, 1963 and 2006. OFFICIAL GAZETTE, FGP 71/52007/2,500 (OL24).

Figueroa, M. & Sives, A. (2003). Garrison politics and criminality in Jamaica: Does the 1997 election represent a turning point? In A. Harriott (Ed.) Understanding crime in Jamaica. Kingston: University of the West Indies Press, pp 63-88.

G

Gayle, H., Grant, A., Bryan, P., Shui, M.L., & Taylor, C. (2004). The adolescents of urban St. Catherine: A study of their reproductive health and survivability. Spanish Town: Children First and UNICEF.

Government of India, Ministry of Urban Development. (2007). Documentation of best practices. New Delhi: Jawaharlal Nehru National Urban Renewal Mission.

Government of Jamaica. (2006). Draft five year strategic plan. Kingston: Board of Supervision.

Government of Jamaica, Ministry of Water and Housing. (2009). The minister of water and housing's budget sectoral debate presentation. Retrieved from: http://www.jis.gov.jm

Government of Jamaica, Ministry of Education and Youth. (2005). National strategic plan for youth 2005-2010. Kingston: Author.

Government of Kenya. (2007). Kenya Vision 2030: The popular version. Retrieved from: http://www.scribd.com/doc/3480381/Vision-2030-Popular-Version

Government of Kenya, Ministry of State for Youth Affairs. (2007b, March). Office of the Vice-President and Ministry of State for Youth Affairs: Strategic plan 2007-2012. Nairobi: Ministry of State for Youth Affairs.

Government of Kenya, Ministry of Planning and National Development. (2007c). Kenya integrated household budget survey 2005/6. Nairobi: Central Bureau of Statistics and Ministry of Planning and National Development.

Government of Kenya, Ministry of Youth Affairs and Sports. (2008). National youth policy. Nairobi: Ministry of State for Youth Affairs.

GUO – UN-HABITAT. (2004). Urban poverty and slums, intra-city differential study of Nairobi. The Urban Observer, 1 (3)

H

Harvey, D. (2006). Spaces of hope. Edinburgh: University of Edinburgh Press.

Hausmann, R., Tyson, L. & Zahidi, S. (2009). Global Gender Gap Report 2009. Geneva: World Economic Forum

Holzmann, R. (2001). Risk and vulnerability: The Forward looking of social protection in a globalizing world. Asia and Pacific Forum on Poverty: Reforming Policies and Institutions for Poverty Reduction, Asian Development Bank, Manila. Retrieved from: http://www.adb.org/Poverty/forum/pdf/Holzmann.pdf

I

ILO. (2005). Resolution concerning youth employment. (Resolution at International Labour Conference, 93rd Session.) Geneva: International Labour Organisation. Retrieved from: http://www.ilo.org/public/english/employment/yett/ilc93.htm

ILO. (2006). Global employment trends for youth. Geneva: International Labour Organisation.

ILO. (2008). Global employment trends for youth. Geneva: International Labour Organisation.

ILO. (2009). Global employment trends. Geneva: International Labour Organisation.

Instituto Pereira Passos, 2008 [Retrieved from http://www.armazemdedados.rio.rj.gov.br]

ISER Assessoria e Observatório Jovem da Universidade Fluminense. (2006). Juventude Brasileira e democracia: Participação, esferas e políticas públicas, relatório regional Rio de Janeiro. Rio de Janeiro: Author.

J

Jimenz, E., Kiso, N., & Ridao-Cano, C. (2007, June). Educational second chances for youth. Development Outreach, 9(2), 20-21.

Jones, G.A. & Chant, S. (2009). Globalising initiatives for gender equality and poverty reduction: Exploring 'failure' with reference to education and work among urban youth in The Gambia and Ghana. Geoforum, 40(2), 184–96.

K

Kahlenberg, R.D. (2004). America's Untapped Resource – Low-Income Students in Higher Education. New York: Century Foundation

Kenya National Bureau of Statistics. (2009). Economic survey 2009. Nairobi: Government Printer.

Kerr, S., Bailey, A. & Knight, P. (2006). The transition of Jamaican youth to the world of work. Kingston: Planning Institute of Jamaica and the International Labour Organisation.

L

Lave, J. (1996). Teaching, as learning, in practice. Mind, Culture, and Activity, 3(3), 149-164.

Lockheed, M. (2008), The double disadvantage of gender and social exclusion in education. In M. Tembon & L. Fort (Eds.), Girls' education in the 21st century: Gender equality, empowerment, and economic growth (pp. 115-126), Washington, D.C.: The World Bank

Luton, D. (2009, 6 May). 'YEP, you can' – Golding launches lending programme for school leavers – lowers interest rates for small, micro and medium-size businesses. Jamaica Gleaner News. Retrieved from: http://www.jamaica-gleaner.com/gleaner/20090506/lead/lead1.html

M

Meeks-Gardner, J., Powell, C., & Grantham-McGregor, S. (2000). A case-control study of family and school determinants of aggression in Jamaican children. Kingston: Planning Institute of Jamaica.

N

National Housing Trust. (n.d.). Annual report and financial statements 2006-2007. Kingston: Author. Retrieved from: http://www.nht.gov.jm

O

Olima, W.H.A. (2001, July). The dynamics and implications of sustaining urban spatial segregation in Kenya: Experiences from Nairobi metropolis. (Lincoln Institute Product Code: CP01A16). Paper prepared for the International Seminar on Segregation in the City at Lincoln Institute of Land Policy, Cambridge, MA.

P

Planning Institute of Jamaica. (2008). Jamaica survey of living conditions 2007. Kingston: Author.

Planning Institute of Jamaica. (2009). Economic and social survey of Jamaica 2008. Kingston: Author.

Planning Institute of Jamaica. (2009). Mapping poverty indicators: Consumption and basic needs in Jamaica 2001/2002. Kingston: Author.

Planning Institute of Jamaica & Ministry of Foreign Affairs and Foreign Trade. (2009, July). National report of Jamaica on Millennium Development Goals for the UN Economic and Social Council annual ministerial review July 2009. Kingston: Author.

Population Reference Bureau. (2009). PRB World's Youth 2006 Data Sheet. Retrieved from: http://www.prb.org/Datafinder/Geography/MultiCompare.aspx?variables=23%2c22&regions=104%2c140%2c93%2c39%2c29%2c

Power K., Varney, D., Ragan, D., & Koernig, K.. (2009, February). Youth in urban Development: Bringing ideas into action. (Working Paper CYE-WP2-2009). Boulder, CO: Children, Youth & Environment Center, University of Colorado.

R

Rio Como Vamos. (2008). Indicadores da cidade. Retrieved from: http://www.riocomovamos.org.br

Roberts, F.O.N. & Oladeji, A. (2001, October). Resurgent Identity Crisis and Security Management in Lagos, Nigeria: Lessons for West African Cities. In Proceedings of International Conference on Security, Segregation and Social Networks in West African Cities, 19th-20th Centuries', Ibadan, Nigeria.

Roemer, E.J. (1998). Equality of opportunity. Cambridge, MA: Harvard University Press.

Roemer, E.J. (2006). Economic development as opportunity equalization. Discussion Paper # 1583. Cowles Foundation for Research in Economics.. New Haven: Yale University.

Rustogi, P. (2009). Paper presented at ILO meeting, July 2009.

S

Samms-Vaughan, M. (2004). The Jamaican pre-school child: The status of early childhood development in Jamaica. Kingston: Planning Institute of Jamaica.

Satyanaryana, V. (2009). Dormitory accomodation for low income workers in India. Paper presented at the UN-HABITAT Business Forum, New Delhi, India.

Sen, A. (1973). On economic inequality. Oxford: Clarendon Press.

Sen, A. (1999). Development as freedom. Oxford: Oxford University Press.

Spence, K. (2006, June). Social development within the inner city housing project. Paper presented at the Conference on Social Housing in the Caribbean, Kingston, Jamaica.

Spinks, C. (2002). Pentecostal Christianity and young Africans. In A. de Waal & N. Argenti (Eds.) Young Africa: Realizing the rights of children and youth. Trenton, NJ: Africa World Press.

Statistical Institute of Jamaica. (2003). Population census: Jamaica 2001. Kingston: Author.

Statistical Institute of Jamaica. (2007). Multiple indicator cluster survey 2005: Monitoring the situation of children and women. Kingston: UNICEF and Statistical Institute of Jamaica.

Statistical Institute of Jamaica. (2009). The labour force 2008. Kingston: Author.

U

Ulack, R. (1978). The role of urban squatter settlements. Annals of the Association of American Geographers, 4(68), 535-550.

UN DESA (2004). World youth report 2003: The global situation of young people. New York: United Nations.

UN DESA. (2005a). World youth report 2005: Young people today and in 2015. New York: United Nations.

UN DESA (2005b). Growing together: Youth and the work of the United Nations. New York: United Nations.

UN DESA. (2005c). World population prospects: The 2004 revision. New York: United Nations.

UN DESA (2007). World Youth Report 2007: Young people's transition to adulthood: Progress and challenges. New York: United Nations.

UN DESA (2008). World Population Prospects: The 2008 Revision. New York: United Nations. Retrieved from: http://esa.un.org/unpp

UNDP (2006). Society and development in crisis? Youth and violent conflict. New York: Author.

UNESCAP (2007) UN Economic and Social Commission for Asia and the Pacific - Economic and Social Survey of Asia and the Pacific 2007 – "Surging Ahead in

Uncertain Times." Bangkok: Retrieved from: http://www.prlog.org/10015642-asia-pacific-region-needs-better-exchange-management.pdf

UNESCO. (2004). Empowering youth through national policies. Paris: Author.

UNESCO. (2007). Education for all by 2015: Will we make it ? Paris: Author.

UNESCO. (2009). Education for all – global monitoring report. Paris: Author.

UNFPA. (2007). State of the world's population report. New York: UN.

UN-HABITAT. (2006a). State of the world's cities report 2006/2007. London: Earthscan.

UN-HABITAT. (2006b). Nairobi urban sector profile. Nairobi: Author.

UN-HABITAT. (2008a). Global Urban Observatory data. Retrieved from: http://www.devinfo.info/urbaninfo.

UN-HABITAT. (2008b). State of the world's cities report 2008/2009: Harmonious cities. London: Earthscan.

UN-HABITAT. (2009). Urban youth survey. Unpublished data collected for UN-HABITAT.

UN-HABITAT. (2010a). State of the world's cities report 2010/2011: Bridging the urban divide. London: Earthscan.

UN-HABITAT. (2010b). Bridging the Urban Gender Divide. Nairobi: Author.

UN-HABITAT. (2010c). Global Urban Indicator Database 2010. Nairobi: Author.

UNICEF. (2007). Progress for children: A world fit for children – Statistical review. New York: Author.

United Nations. (2002a). "Gender mainstreaming: An Overview" New York: Author.

United Nations. (2002b). General Assembly resolution on promoting youth employment, A/RES/57/165. Retrieved from: http://www.un.org/esa/socdev/unyin/library.htm#otherdocuments.

United Nations. (2004, January). General Assembly resolution on policies and programmes involving youth, A/RES/58/133. Retrieved from: http://www.un.org/esa/socdev/unyin/library.htm#otherdocuments.

V

Viva Rio & Innovations in Civic Participation. (2005). Youth service: A policy for preventing and providing alternatives to youth involvement in urban violence in Brazil. Retrieved from: http://www.icicp.org/ht/a/GetDocumentAction/i/2726

W

Wolff, E.N. (2001). Skills, Computerization, and Earnings in the Postwar U.S. Economy. Levy Economics Institute, The Economics Working Paper Archive # 331. Retrieved from: http://129.3.20.41/eps/mac/papers/0106/0106007.pdf

World Bank. (n.d.). World Bank staff estimates based on primary household survey data obtained from government statistical agencies and World Bank country departments. For more information and methodology, see PovcalNet (http://iresearch.worldbank.org/PovcalNet/jsp/index.jsp).

World Bank. (2005). World Development Indicators (WDI) online database. Retrieved from: http://web.worldbank.org/WBSITE/EXTERNAL/DATASTATISTICS/0,,contentMDK:20398986~menuPK:64133163~pagePK:64133150~piPK:64133175~theSitePK:239419,00.html

World Bank. (2006). World development report 2007: Development and the next generation. Washington, D.C.: Author.

World Bank. (2008). Kenya poverty and inequality assessment. (Draft report, Volume I). Washington, D.C.: World Bank.

World Bank. (2009). World Development Indicators (WDI) online database. Retrieved from: http://web.worldbank.org/WBSITE/EXTERNAL/DATASTATISTICS/0,,contentMDK:20398986~menuPK:64133163~pagePK:64133150~piPK:64133175~theSitePK:239419,00.html

World Charter. (2005). World Charter on the Right to the City. Retrieved from: http://portal.unesco.org/shs/en/ev.php-URL_ID=8218&URL_DO=DO_TOPIC&URL_SECTION=201.HTML

Appendix

National and Local Youth Policies in the Five Cities under review

A. National Youth Policies and City Youth Perception Responses

A common feature of the five cities under review in this Report is that they belong in countries with national youth policies. In Brazil, *Pro-Jovem* (pro-youth) has supported youth inclusion at national and municipal levels since 2005. Jamaica revised its own 1994 National Youth Policy in 2001, two years before India launched her own and seven years before Kenya. Nigeria revised its 1989 national youth policy in 1999. Kenya drew up its national youth policy in 2008. In the excerpts from reports drawn up by urban experts, available youth programmes are described below.

Mumbai, India

In India, one of the earliest youth-specific initiatives was launched in 1972 under the Ministry of Education. A department of youth affairs was established in 1985. In 1988, the Indian government adopted a National Youth Policy with the following three main objectives:

- "promoting awareness of the country's historical and cultural heritage among youth;"

- developing "qualities of discipline, self-reliance and justice and promoting a scientific frame of mind;"

- ensuring young people's "full access to education and training".

The Youth Department became a full-fledged ministry in the year 2000, with two independent directorates, one for youth affairs and the other for sports. The Nehru Yuvak Kendra Sanghatana (NYKS) became an implementing body for youth policy. In effect, it is mostly a vocational and life skills training institute.

Under this policy, a Plan of Action was adopted in 1992. The main programmes have strengthened educational opportunities and supported entrepreneurial endeavours. The practical outcomes included youth hostels, sports infrastructure, award schemes, training and coaching facilities, grants to sports associations and encouraging sports in schools and colleges.

> **Young voices from Mumbai:**
>
> - India's Youth Policy should be participatory and more programme-oriented, allowing each state and city to develop complementary plans.
>
> - Interest in participating in public affairs is poor because of lack of time, not because nothing could be done to change things.
>
> - Municipal reforms and policies are of benefit only to politicians, bureaucrats and the young rich.
>
> - Every state and city should address region- and city-specific issues, such as ensuring adequate, decent housing and improved quality of employment in Mumbai.
>
> - The country's sports policy must be reformed to integrate and reflect youth policies, so that provision of open spaces becomes as important as providing world-class sporting arenas. There should be funding and other support for massive improvement programmes in sports through schools and clubs, rather than only individual scholarships. Planning of mega-events in sports should involve youth participation.
>
> - High schools are often further from homes than primary schools, and girls typically tend to be withdrawn at the higher levels because they have to travel great distances to school. The consequence is that even though in Mumbai (as in all of Maharashtra state) girls' education has been free of charge up to the higher secondary stage, girls continue to drop out of high school because of access problems.

In 2003 India adopted a new, substantially different National Youth Policy with a broader perspective on youth development. The new policy focuses on four main areas:

i. Youth empowerment;

ii. Gender justice;

iii. Cross-sector approaches; and

iv. Information and research networks.

In order to facilitate cross-sector approaches, the policy suggests that "all ministries of the state and Union governments should make identifiable budget allocations for youth development programmes". Currently, 12 such schemes are under implementation. In 2003, an assessment gave all programmes "poor" to "average" ratings on all counts.

While no comprehensive evaluation of the policy and the programmes is available, commentators tend to concur that India's youth-related ministries efforts to deploy specific programmes have been inadequate. Indeed, within the dedicated ministry of youth affairs and sports, the sports department claimed 88 per cent of the 2008/09 allocated budget.

In India's federal structure, the legislative function is shared between individual states and the Union. This is the case with health and education, whereas sport is a state responsibility. Setting up coordinating bodies across ministries has always been recognizably difficult in India. Each federated state should ideally formulate its own youth policy reflecting the national policy. This has happened only in a few states.

Rio de Janeiro, Brazil

In Brazil, policies aimed at vulnerable youth over the past decade assumed that the large number of unemployed young people could be behind the country's high degrees of violence, further stigmatizing the younger population (defined in Brazil as aged between 15 and 29).

In 2003, a "National Programme to Encourage First Employment for Youth" was launched with the objective of promoting "the qualification of youth for the job market and social inclusion, as well as the creation of work placements for young people or to prepare them for the job market and alternative gainful employment". The target group was those aged 16 to 24 who were unemployed or had no experience of formal employment, who had not completed basic education and whose family's income was no higher than one minimum salary per head. The programme offers subsidies to companies that hire young apprentices.

In 2004, Brazil's "Programme for Education, Culture and Citizenship" (known as *Pontos de Cultura*) sought to remedy deficiencies in the education system. Its aim is to promote access to information and cultural expression through special teaching methods in suburbs, small municipalities and *favelas*, financing local initiatives with an emphasis on children and young people.

Since 2005, this policy is backed up by a National Youth Secretariat, which coordinates the implementation of programmes by no less than 19 different government departments. The policy is based on six principles:

- The singularity of youth: Youth cannot be considered as a short transition phase between childhood and adulthood. Young men and women come with their own individual potentials as well as specific needs and demands, calling for specific policies to improve their current living conditions and prepare them for the future.

- Protection of youth rights: The rationale is to emancipate young people rather than control the lives of young men and women. Youth should have opportunities to put their capacities to productive, fulfilling use. Government should offer services that guarantee basic conditions for the realization of young men and women's basic needs and development.

- Valuing youth diversity: Public authorities recognize that 50.5 million of young people in a continental and multicultural country like Brazil feature innumerable differences in terms of identity, forms of organization and expression. Diversity must be valued and inequalities reduced.

- Support to the most vulnerable: The National Youth Policy focuses on universal policies for all, but does not overlook the more vulnerable.

- Integration of policies: Education, work, health, sport, culture and the environment are not separate areas in the lives of young men and women. Government should guarantee that although various ministries are involved in policy implementation, all projects are integrated.

- Youth participation: Government should create the conditions required for enhanced participation and dialogue with youth movements. Conversely, youth should take an active role in designing, monitoring and evaluating policies.

- *Pro-Jovem* is the single main plank in Brazil's youth policies, which also involves 16 other programmes focusing on formal education, healthcare, leisure, culture, sports and the environment.

- As Brazil's national programme for the inclusion of young people since 2005, Pro-Jovem features four main components:

i) *ProJovem Urban* is aimed at young people between 18 and 29 who are out of school and have not completed basic education, but are literate. The scheme helps them complete basic education, and provides job training schemes and computing courses.

ii) *ProJovem Worker* targets unemployed young people who are in middle or basic education or youth education courses, and are members of families with incomes of up to one minimum salary per head. The objective is to prepare young people for the job market and alternative gainful activities with professional qualifications, life skills and extra schooling.

iii) *Pro-Jovem Adolescent* encourages socially vulnerable school drop-outs aged 15-17 to return to school and ensure that their families receive basic social assistance and protection, regardless of income.

iv) Pro-Jovem Rural is executed at local level by municipal authorities and supervised by local committees. The scheme offers professional qualifications that match municipal needs.

In Brazil, youth-specific public policies are developed by various tiers of government – federal, state and municipal – but are implemented mostly at local level through partnerships between public authorities and civil society.

Young voices from Rio de Janeiro:

- Government policy hands over youth-dedicated resources to non-governmental organizations. But young people point out that the courses on offer under government policies are either insufficient or sporadic and out of touch with the market.

- Youth demand affirmative action in employment, as happens with some banks that set themselves quotas for hiring people with disabilities and blacks.

- While there are good initiatives, coordination of existing projects and programmes is lacking, as is political will, or so it seems, to improve conditions for this segment of the population. "I don't think that it is just a matter of competence, I think it is a lack of political will. We have competence, what is lacking is the will to see things through."

- Housing policies in general do not offer any specific schemes for young people. It takes a very long time for them to be able to purchase a house. The young claim that although there are many programmes, none really meet their needs, especially those least privileged who hardly ever have a steady income. Young people also note that affordable housing in general is of poor quality.

- Policies that allow youth half price entrance to cultural events are good but there is talk of restricting their scope.

- As implemented at the local level, the Pro-Jovem programme earned praise in principle, but some young people stated that beneficiaries were not always those who most needed it.

Nairobi, Kenya

Kenya's Ministry of Youth Affairs and Sports (MOYAS) was established in 2005 to promote young people's capacity to participate in national development through supportive policies and programmes. Youth policy priorities include employment, empowerment, health and access to education, training, technologies and recreation services. The MOYAS mandate also includes:

- Coordination of youth organizations' networks.

- The development of youth resource centres.

- Strengthening polytechnic colleges and the National Youth Service.

- Promotion and development of sports and related facilities.

- Support to the establishment of a National Youth Council.

Kenya's National Youth Policy (2008) considers the eight following areas as requiring attention in order to promote youth interests : (1) employment creation; (2) health; (3) education and training; (4) recreation, leisure and community service; (5) the environment; (6) crime and drug abuse; (7) the media and ICTs (information and communication technologies); and (8) empowerment and participation in national life. Kenya's youth policy has also categorized young people into priority target groups: youth with disabilities; street youth; youth infected with HIV/Aids; female youth; unemployed youth; and out of school youth.

The policy recommends that an Act of Parliament establish a National Youth Council for effective implementation. The Council will co-ordinate youth organizations, review the National Youth Policy on an ongoing basis and develop an "integrated national youth development plan" in collaboration with the Ministry for Youth Affairs. The *Kenya National Youth Council Bill* was tabled in Parliament for a first reading in May 2009. In January 2010, the President of Kenya finally signed the Law establishing the National Youth Council. This Council will ensure the inclusion of the youth agenda in formulation of policy by institutions; and also promote their inclusion in decision making bodies.

In the meantime, a number of other policies and programmes could be targeted at inequalities if implemented with a youth focus. They include:

- The Nairobi Metro-2030 plan: The strategy laid out by the Ministry of Nairobi Metropolitan Development (2008) features "enhancing the quality of life and inclusiveness" as one of its objectives.

- The Sessional Paper on Micro-, Small- and Medium-size Enterprises and Vision 2030 provides a framework for the upgrading of the informal sector's provision of skills training and jobs to youth, but resources and implementation have not shown any urban youth focus to date.

In 2009, MOYAS launched its *"Kazi kwa Vijana"* (work for young people), initiative, under which young people can be employed in community projects (water harvesting, repairing boreholes and roads, cleaning informal settlements, planting trees, etc.). The programme aims to stem the social ills brought about by unemployment, idleness and poverty. However, the jobs are temporary and labour-intensive, and many put females at a disadvantage.

The first Medium-Term Plan (2008-2012) laid out under the Vision 2030 framework recommends a comprehensive review of laws relating to decentralization of funds. If this were to become effective, access to resources could be improved at the local level in favour of excluded groups.

Young voices from Nairobi:

- The government must provide a place where young people can go to for assistance.

- Government tells us there is a Youth Fund but they don't tell us where it is. I am told that to access the Fund you must know Members of Parliament (MPs). I don't know my MP.

- Vision 2030 is supposed to be for us. But we don't know the details. I know they are talking about it in the media, but they do not ask us about it.

- Politicians are interested in young people only at election time. They give us 500 shillings [or just under 7 US dollars] each and we believe it is the best thing ever. It is for young people to realize the power they can have. The things politicians promised during election campaigns, they have not delivered any of them. We must find channels to hold them accountable.

- The politicians in Kenya are selfish. They don't listen to anybody except themselves. Even if young people have opinions about something, we sometimes do not bother as we wonder who will listen to us anyway.

- To some extent, some politicians are working for our good. I am talking about people that I know. A youth group went to meet a certain MP and he was able to engage with them.

Lagos, Nigeria

Nigeria first launched a national youth policy in 1983 and revised it in 1989, 1999 and then again in 2001. However, the policy has yet to be endorsed and enacted in all the states of the Nigerian federation. The Ministry of Inter-Governmental Affairs, Youth and Special Duties was also established in 1999. But this recognition of youth as an important element in national development has yet to be endorsed by individual federated states.

The government of Lagos state has shown concern for youth through a "Support Our Schools" initiative aimed at raising standards. On top of providing free education in 1,030 primary schools, 313 junior secondary schools and 303 senior secondary schools in the state, Lagos has waived all examination fees in public schools and re-equipped science laboratories. The government of Lagos recognizes the Lagos State Youth Forum as a Chapter of the National Youth Council of Nigeria, a forum that serves as a bridge between youth and the government. Lagos state is also rehabilitating and constructing sports facilities, offering micro-credit and deploying youth employment schemes.

Young voices from Lagos:

- Planning takes place at all three tiers of government. Whenever where there are plans, functions like monitoring and evaluation of the degree and extent of implementation are never in place.

- The autonomy enjoyed by each of the lower tiers of government provides leeway for lack of connections between the different programmes implemented by each of them. The problem basically is with leaders, whose selfish interests override national interest and benefits.

- The (national) leader's political party has programmes which the party expects all the states whose governor is a member to implement, regardless of whether these programmes reflect the interests of constituents.

- No reduction in urban youth poverty is expected, not just for lack of initiative or continuity in programmes, but also because the government does not involve young people in programme design and has no plan to alter the seemingly bleak future that lies ahead of them.

- Even though some young people are paraded in the media to illustrate their social inclusion, they never represent the true interests of the country's youths.

- Public transport used to be very unreliable and expensive, but since the advent of the state government's public transport service, the situation has improved tremendously.

Kingston, Jamaica

In 1994, the Jamaican government developed a national Youth Policy to empower young people aged 14 to 25. In the year 2000, the National Centre for Youth Development (NCYD) was set up to ensure effective coordination of, and collaboration on, youth-related programmes and research and to act as an information clearinghouse, a priority identified by the 1994 policy. In 2004, a five-year (2005-2009) youth policy was developed, serving as the basis for implementation of the National Youth Policy.

A national survey is planned ahead of the development of a new, 2010-2014 youth policy. The revision process is participatory, with youth organizations involved together with other non-governmental organizations and government agencies. The areas of relevance to youth come under proactive discussion. They include crime, violence, teenage pregnancy and parenting, gender disparities and young people's role in national unity. The new youth policy is to focus on the following areas:

- Education and training.
- Employment and entrepreneurship.
- Health.
- Participation and empowerment.
- Care and protection.
- Living environments.
- Leisure (sports, music, etc.).

In the meantime, Jamaica's other youth-supportive policies and programmes include the following:

- The National Centre operates five Youth Information Centres; these youth-friendly spaces allow young people to feel comfortable discussing and accessing information on issues concerning them.

- Action for the Rights of Children and Young People. The 2004 Child Care and Protection Act introduced new standards for treatment. The Act makes not just government but every citizen accountable and responsible for reporting incidents of child abuse, and failing to do so is punishable by law.

- The High School Equivalency Programme is a secondary education scheme that targets people over 18 years who have not completed secondary education or lack adequate certification for higher education. The scheme, which has just been launched, represents a shift in focus from traditional learning (classroom teaching) to independent, self-directed learning, using self-instructional material.

- In 2007 the Jamaican government abolished secondary education tuition fees. No child can be legally turned away if parents are unable to pay the additional support fees, which are voluntary.

Despite these policies and programmes, disturbing negative evolutions are taking place in Jamaica, such as stronger networking among inner-city gangs, and persistent rises in the numbers of school drop-outs among boys and girls raised by single mothers or orphaned through urban violence.

Young voices from Kingston:

- The problem persists because we feel the government must come to us before we go to them, as opposed to taking the initiative into our own hands and becoming united as a group and moving forward. We need to move there.

- We need to assume 100% responsibility and become proactive. A lot of people are fed up and they must start taking action.

- One might be qualified for a job, but because someone wants their friend to get it they will give it to them, whether or not they are as qualified.

- Corruption is even more of an issue during election time; guns are traded for votes and people can be killed for voting for a party that their community does not support, or for deciding not to vote.

- I wouldn't know who to vote for, I don't trust either (party), I feel like they're lying.

STATE OF THE URBAN YOUTH 2010/2011

LEVELING THE PLAYING FIELD

Half of humankind is now under 25 years of age and largely urban, and yet youth exclusion features as a major aspect of the "urban divide" that gives its theme to UN-HABITAT's State of the World Cities 2010/2011. This companion Report, the first of its kind, focuses on the dynamics of youth exclusion currently at work in four developing regions.

This State of the Urban Youth 2010/2011 report combines the latest academic and policy research with new statistics from UN-HABITAT' Global Urban Observatory. The perceptions of over 700 youth in five representative cities, as collected through a survey and local discussion groups, help pinpoint the factors behind unequal opportunities in the economic, social, political and cultural spheres.

The Report finds that predetermined circumstances like gender, parents' education and location influence inequality of opportunity among young people, and that good-quality education is a major factor of equality. Another major finding is that higher school enrolment ratios boost economic growth some 15 years down the road, although improved literacy rates do not always result in proportional job opportunities for all.

Unequal opportunities call for a more level playing field for urban youth. This Report recommends enhanced awareness of youth issues among policymakers at all levels of government, so that policies espouse the multidimensional nature of youth opportunity. Special emphasis must be laid on good-quality education, particularly for young females. Protection of youth must combine with the promotion of their voice and empowerment if they are to move to the kind of responsible, fulfilling citizenship that will help shape a better collective future for all.

9789211320107
STATE OF THE URBAN YOUTH: 2010

publishing for a sustainable future